Timo Schläfer

Recovery Risk in Credit Default Swap Premia

GABLER RESEARCH

Timo Schläfer

Recovery Risk in Credit Default Swap Premia

GABLER

RESEARCH

Bibliographic information published by the Deutsche Nationalbibliothek
The Deutsche Nationalbibliothek lists this publication in the Deutsche Nationalbibliografie; detailed bibliographic data are available in the Internet at http://dnb.d-nb.de.

Dissertation Karlsruhe Institute of Technology, 2010

1st Edition 2011

Editorial Office: Stefanie Brich | Anita Wilke

Gabler Verlag is a brand of Springer Fachmedien.
Springer Fachmedien is part of Springer Science+Business Media.
www.gabler.de

Cover design: KünkelLopka Medienentwicklung, Heidelberg
Printed on acid-free paper
Printed in Germany

ISBN 978-3-8349-2844-3

Preface

This study developed during my time as an external postgraduate student at the Chair of Financial Engineering and Derivatives at the Karlsruhe Institute of Technology (KIT) and was accepted by the KIT as Ph.D. thesis. I sincerely thank my advisor Prof. Dr. Marliese Uhrig-Homburg for the outstanding support during that time. Despite her own busy schedule, she was always highly approachable when I needed guidance or input. Without her feedback and suggestions, this study would not have achieved the level of quality it has now.

Further, I would like to thank my co-advisor Prof. Dr. Christof Weinhardt for his interest in my work, Prof. Dr. Martin Ruckes for acting as an examiner, and Prof. Dr. Jan Kowalski for chairing the board of examiners.

I am also much indebted to my former colleagues at Goldman Sachs, in particular Fabian Brügmann, who provided me with some of the data. Without their generous support, much of my empirical work would not have been feasible in its present form.

Finally, my thanks go to my colleagues and friends at the Chair of Financial Engineering and Derivatives, in particular Nils Unger, whose profound mathematical knowledge proved a valuable resource and Michael Kunisch, who helped me greatly on several occasions.

This book is dedicated to my parents, to whom I am grateful for their unconditional support.

Timo Schläfer

Table of Contents

List of Figures

List of Tables

List of Abbreviations

APR	Absolute priority rule
BP	Basis point
CDS	Credit default swap
CD	Certificate of deposit
CLO	Collateralized loan obligation
EBITDA	Earnings before interest, tax, depreciation, and amortization
GDP	Gross domestic product
IG	Investment grade
ISDA	International Swaps and Derivatives Organization
LBO	Leveraged buyout
LCDS	Loan-only credit default swap
LIBOR	London Interbank Offered Rate
M&A	Mergers and acquisitions
MMR	Modified modified restructuring
MR	Modified restructuring
OR	Old restructuring
OTC	Over-the-counter
RMSE	Root mean squared error
RR	Recovery rate
U.S.-GAAP	United States Generally Accepted Accounting Principles
XR	No restructuring

List of Symbols

a	Percentage share of senior secured loans in a borrower's total liabilities
$\alpha_0, \dots, \alpha_2$	Shape parameters for the quadratic distribution
$A_t(T)$	Time t value of an annuity paying one until τ or T, whichever comes first
b	Percentage share of senior secured loans plus senior secured bonds in a borrower's total liabilities
$B_t(T)$	Time t value of the default-free zero coupon bond with maturity T
$bet(\cdot)$	Probability density of the beta distribution
$\beta_0, \dots, \beta_8$	Constant regression parameters
c	Percentage share of senior secured loans plus senior secured bonds plus senior unsecured bonds in a borrower's total liabilities
$C(\cdot)$	Confluent hypergeometric function
CDX	CDX High-Yield
e	Upper boundary for the ratio of firm value to liabilities at default
ε	Positive, arbitrarily small constant
F	(L)CDS notional principal
F_IntCov	Firm-specific interest rate coverage ratio
F_Lev	Firm-specific financial leverage
F_Quick	Firm-specific quick ratio
F_Tan	Firm-specific asset tangibility
γ_0, γ_1	Constant regression parameters
$h(\cdot)$	Probability density of recovery given default
η	Coefficient of risk aversion
I	Number of firms in Sample 1
I_Diss	Industry distress
I_Illiq	Industry illiquidity
I_Lev	Industry financial leverage

$instr$, $instr^-$, $instr^+$	Percentage share of debt of a given seniority in a borrower's total liabilities, percentage share of debt ranking relatively junior, relatively senior
J	Number of firms in Sample 2
jr, jr^-, jr^+	Percentage share of junior debt in a borrower's total liabilities, percentage share of debt ranking relatively junior, relatively senior
$loan$	Percentage share of senior secured loans in a borrower's total liabilities
λ_t	Instantaneous default arrival rate at time t
μ	Mean of the probability density of recovery given default
$\bar{\mu}$	Shape parameter for the transformed normal distribution
M_t	Value of a money market investment of one at time t
$N(\cdot)$	Cumulative normal distribution
p	Shape parameter for the beta distribution
P	Physical probability measure
$P_t(\cdot)$	Value of the (L)CDS premium leg at time t
PD	One-year probability of default
$PR_t(\cdot)$	Value of the (L)CDS protection leg at time t
q	Shape parameter for the beta distribution
Q	Risk-neutral probability measure
$\tilde{Q}$	T-forward probability measure
r_t	Instantaneous risk-free rate at time t
R, R_1, R_2	Actual ratio of premia, ratio of senior unsecured CDSs and senior subordinated CDSs, ratio of LCDSs and senior unsecured CDSs
$\bar{R}, \bar{R}_1, \bar{R}_2$	Model-implied ratio of premia, ratio of senior unsecured CDSs and senior subordinated CDSs, ratio of LCDSs and senior unsecured CDSs
ρ^Q	Short for $E^Q[\rho \mid 1_{\{\tau \le T\}} = 1]$
ρ, ρ_{firm}, ρ_{instr}, ρ_{jr}, ρ_{loan}, ρ_{uns}, ρ_{sr}, ρ_{sub}	Default-conditional recovery rate at time T, of the entire firm, of debt of a given seniority, of a junior obligation, of senior secured loans, of senior unsecured bonds, of a senior obligation, of senior subordinated bonds
s, s_{jr}, s_{loan}, s_{uns}, s_{sr}, s_{sub}	Premium of a (L)CDS, referencing a junior obligation, a senior secured loan, a senior unsecured bond, a senior obligation, a senior subordinated bond
S	Price of the borrower's stock

sec	Percentage share of senior secured bonds in a borrower's total liabilities
sr, sr^{-}, sr^{+}	Percentage share of senior debt in a borrower's total liabilities, percentage share of debt ranking relatively junior, relatively senior
sub	Percentage share of senior subordinated bonds in a borrower's total liabilities
σ, σ_{inf}, σ_{sup}, σ_{prem}	Absolute standard deviation of the probability density of recovery given default, infimum of σ for a given μ, supremum of σ for a given μ, excess σ over σ_{inf}
$\bar{\sigma}$	Shape parameter for the transformed normal distribution
$t(\cdot)$	Probability density of the transformed normal distribution
T	Time to maturity
T_n	Number of observed pairs of premia for firm n
ϑ_0, ϑ_1	Constant parameter
τ	Time of default
$u(\cdot)$	Probability density of the quadratic distribution
$U(\cdot)$	Utility-of-wealth-function of the representative agent
uns	Percentage share of senior unsecured bonds in a borrower's total liabilities
$V_t(\cdot)$	Value of a defaultable zero coupon bond at time t
w, w_0	Wealth, initial wealth of the representative agent
x	Ratio of firm value to liabilities at default
$X(\cdot)$	Payment to the investor if default occurs in $\tau \leq T$
ξ_0, ξ_1	Constant parameters

1 Introduction

Research on the determinants of recovery in default shows that there is a systematic component in recovery risk and that in times of financial distress and rising default rates, recovery rates tend to be particularly low. This has important ramifications for credit risk management and stress testing: Altman, Brady, Resti, and Sironi (2005) estimate that assuming constant recovery rates or independence from systematic factors underestimates value at risk, and hence economic capital, by approximately 30%. In its framework documentation on capital measurement and capital standards (Basel II), the Basel Committee on Banking Supervision accordingly demands that recovery estimates "reflect economic downturn conditions where necessary to capture the relevant risks"[1].

Market-implied recovery rates, whilst not directly conveying real-world expectations, concern the subject of risk management as well, albeit in a more subtle manner: In addition to the above, the provisions of Basel II require that "if recovery rates are negatively related to default rates, loss given default parameters must embed forecasts of future recovery rates that are lower than expected during more neutral conditions"[2]. For instance, in summer 2008 it was unambiguous that a major financial crisis was under way and that the months to come might see a considerable number of default events and possibly lower-than-average recovery rates. In such an environment the risk manager is thus obliged to reduce estimates of future physical recovery rates accordingly, but deciding just how substantial such an adjustment should reasonably be is at her own discretion. Historical recovery rates are of little help in answering this question: They are backward-looking by definition and only if data for comparable situations is available can they serve as a basis to infer reasonable assumptions. Implied recovery rates, on the other hand, carry information as to the market's expectation of future economic conditions. Analyzing how changes in these expectations have affected implied figures can thus provide more precise an indication of how model parameters need be altered to adequately account for current risks.

Reliable estimates of implied recovery rates are furthermore indispensable for the pricing of many credit-risky assets, although practitioners frequently use comparable actual realizations as a substitute. For instance, senior unsecured bonds have historically recovered around 40% and this figure is oftentimes used as a proxy for the implied expected recovery rate of credit

---

1 Basel Committee on Banking Supervision (2006), §468.
2 Basel Committee on Banking Supervision (2005), p2.

default swaps (CDSs) on these bonds. This practice, however, is problematic for at least three reasons. First, if the dynamics of implied recovery rates are similar to those observed under the physical measure, i.e. if figures are lower in downturns and vice versa, using a constant input factor will generally under-price the CDS in times of distress and generally over-price it if the economy fares well. Second, Le (2007) notes that employing historical observations does not adequately reflect the market's expectation of the future economic development. As mentioned earlier, implied estimates are forward-looking and thus more apt for this purpose. Third and maybe most importantly, if recovery risk is systematic and hence not diversifiable, investors will require a premium for bearing this risk such that implied expected recovery rates will on average be lower than comparable physical realizations. Güntay, Madan, and Unal (2003) and Pan and Singleton (2008) remark that using historical recovery rates for asset pricing therefore assumes risk-neutrality and disregards the risks involved.

Understanding the characteristics of implied recovery rates should therefore be of interest to a variety of market participants, be it risk managers, traders, or developers of forward-looking credit risk models. Efforts to the end of enhancing this understanding are, however, exacerbated importantly by an identification problem known since Jarrow and Turnbull (1995) and Duffie and Singleton (1999): In most approaches to credit risk modeling, default and loss rates are essentially multiplicatively linked, complicating a separate identification of either factor. Prior studies concerned with the extraction of implied recovery rates negotiate this hurdle only by employing rather implausible assumptions. Specifically, these are either i) constant implied recovery rates, ii) an explicit, arbitrarily imposed relationship between (stochastic) implied default and recovery rates or iii) independence between the two. These characteristics are at odds with what is known about recovery under the physical measure, and it thus is questionable whether implied dynamics are accounted for appropriately.

It is the objective of this thesis to devise a robust, assumption-light approach to estimating implied recovery rates from CDS premia that delivers reliable, economically meaningful estimation outcomes. To this end, two peculiarities in the cash flows of CDSs are exploited: First, the protection seller receives a payment only in the event the reference entity defaults but not otherwise. This is different from the structure of other credit-risky assets, such as bonds, under which payments can occur in either case. Second, the present value of the CDS premium payments is a function only of the implied probability of default but not of the implied expected recovery rate. If the CDS pricing equation is formulated under the T-forward measure, these two properties allow it to isolate interest rate risk, default risk, and recovery risk without assuming independence between any of these factors. As a result, it can be shown that the ratio of premia of two CDSs referencing a junior and a senior debt instrument of a given issuer, respectively, is a function only of the implied expected recovery rates of these two instruments but not of the implied probability of default. The identification problem is thus overcome in an elegant manner, and rigid presuppositions such as those employed by earlier studies are eschewed.

In a second step, issuers' capital structure is analyzed such that, based on the priority of claims, a relation between the ratio of firm value to liabilities at default and instrument-specific recovery rates can be established. Calibrating model parameters to market data then permits estimating the entire probability distribution of recovery conditional on default for a particular firm at a particular point in time. The mean and the standard deviation of this distribution are allowed to vary stochastically and no parametric relationship to the implied probability of default is imposed.

The practical implementation of this method is illustrated using CDSs referencing senior unsecured and senior subordinated bonds as well as loan-only credit default swaps (LCDSs), an altogether new asset class. LCDSs share the purpose of "traditional" CDSs in that they allow trading the credit risk associated with some debt obligation but are intended for use with leveraged loans as opposed to bonds. Leveraged loans are senior secured loans of sub-investment grade issuers and usually rank senior to all other debt of a borrower. Thus, debt of three distinct seniorities is employed in the estimation procedure, setting the analysis on a broad and stable basis.

The results of this thesis add manifold to the existing literature on implied recovery and shed light on several aspects of the topic that have hitherto not been examined at all or only in considerable less detail. Particular emphasis is on finding answers to the following questions:

- How are implied recovery rates related to firm-specific and industry-specific factors and what is their reaction to changes in the economic environment?
- How do debt cushion effects influence implied instrument-specific recovery rates in theory and in practice?
- How do average historical recovery rates compare to implied estimates and what does this relation reveal about the premium for taking recovery risk?
- Can estimates of implied recovery be used to deduce the implied probability of default and what is the relation of both factors under the pricing measure?

To prepare the ground for this program, Chapter 2 commences with a summary of what is known about recovery under the physical measure. This brings first insights into the general characteristics of recovery rates and later allows setting estimation results into perspective. Next, the difficulties associated with a separation of implied default and recovery rates are illustrated using the example of a defaultable zero coupon bond, followed by a survey of how earlier research tackled this issue. Particular attention is being paid to the methods and assumptions employed therein, and, based on the foregone discussion of physical realizations, the plausibility of results is assessed.

Chapter 3 then develops the approach pursued in this thesis, showing how recovery information can be extracted from pairs of CDSs on corporate debt. To the end of identifying suitable instruments for a practical implementation, Chapter 4 gives an overview of common types of CDSs and discusses potential combinations. This makes it necessary to compare in detail the properties of CDSs and LCDSs such that divergent contract specification can be properly accounted for.

Chapter 5 first describes the data and details the empirical specification of the model as well as the calibration procedure. Thereafter, estimation results are presented and the characteristics of implied recovery rates are examined from various vantage points. Robustness is assessed through two alternative model parameterizations, a different approach to calibrating the model, and by comparing implied estimates to historical realizations. Next, estimates of implied recovery rates are used to deduce implied probabilities of default and the relation of both factors under the pricing measure is examined. Again, historical estimates are employed to set implied estimates into perspective.

Finally, Chapter 6 summarizes the principal findings and concludes with suggestions for future research. The ideas and results presented in Chapters 3 and 5 are taken in large part from Schläfer and Uhrig-Homburg (2010b). Chapter 4 is a synopsis of Schläfer and Uhrig-Homburg (2010a).

2 Related Literature

Early research on credit-risky assets mostly concentrated on default arrival risk, and only relatively little attention was being paid to other aspects of the subject. This has changed dramatically throughout the last decade or so, and in particular recovery risk has moved in the focus of practitioners and researchers alike. Any endeavor to further enhance the understanding of this topic should therefore not go without a thorough review of prior research.

Section 2.1 commences with a survey of what is known about recovery under the physical measure. In this context, it is of particular interest to see where recovery rates have come out historically as well as to understand their determinants and how they are related to physical default rates. Section 2.2 then uses the example of a defaultable zero coupon bond to illustrate the obstacles associated with separating implied default and recovery rates. Second, earlier approaches to estimating implied recovery are delineated such that the methodology of this thesis can be put in perspective.

2.1 Characteristics of Physical Recovery Rates

It is well-known that recovery in default is strongly affected by the ranking of an obligation and the assets securing it, with senior and well-collateralized instruments typically recovering significantly more than junior and/or unsecured obligations. To illustrate this, Figure 2.1 shows historical recovery rates for different types of debt issued by corporates and financial institutions worldwide. Data are taken from selected studies and refer to trading prices approximately 30 days after default.[3] Mean recovery rates are highest for senior secured loans (average across all studies: 66%), followed by senior secured bonds (53%), senior unsecured bonds (40%), senior subordinated bonds (32%), and junior subordinated bonds (31%). It is remarkable that figures are much different for senior secured loans and senior secured bonds, despite both being "senior" and "secured". It will be argued in Chapter 4 that this is due to the covenant-heavy design of senior secured loans as well as to inter-creditor agreements typically attributing a higher priority to claims of loan holders.

[3] Trading prices after default reflect the market's risk-adjusted expectation of ultimate recovery rates on defaulted obligations. Ultimate recovery rates are determined only after the claims of all creditors as well as the issuer's remaining assets have been assessed and possible disputes have been resolved, a process that often lasts several years. In this thesis, physical recovery rates always refer to trading prices after default.

Figure 2.1 also shows the standard deviation of recovery rates for each type of debt. Numbers are higher for senior unsecured bonds than for all other asset classes, including the riskier subordinated bonds. This is explainable with recovery rates being confined to a limited interval[4], inducing an interdependency between their mean and standard deviation. The discussion in Section 3.3 shows that, ceteris paribus, the standard deviation of recovery rates is therefore particularly low for the more junior and senior asset classes.

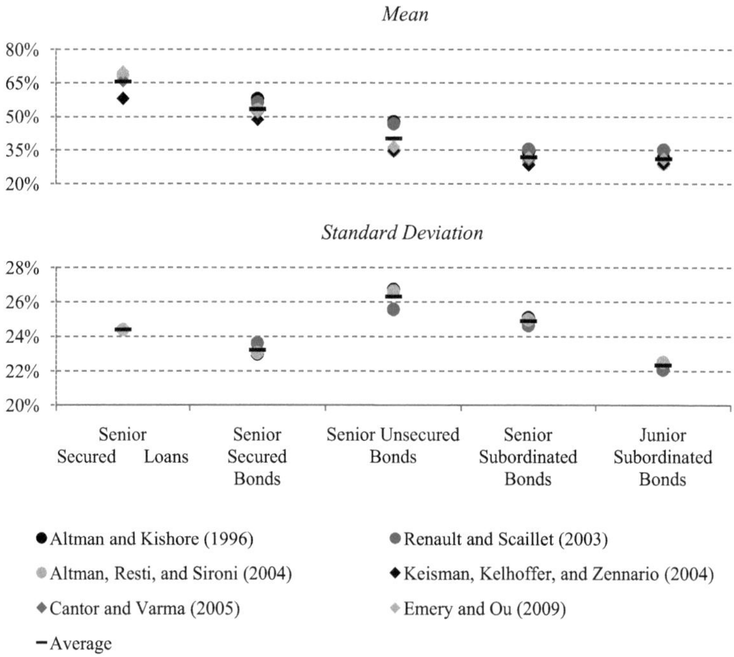

Figure 2.1: Historical Recovery Rates by Type of Debt
This figure illustrates the mean and the standard deviation of historically realized recovery rates (defined as trading prices approximately 30 days after default) for different types of debt issued by corporates and financial institutions worldwide. Data sources and observation periods are as follows: Altman and Kishore (1996): proprietary database, 1978 to 1995; Renault and Scaillet (2003): S&P/Portfolio Management Data LLC, 1981 to 1999; Altman, Resti, and Sironi (2004): Moody's for loans, proprietary database for bonds, 1989 to 2003 for loans and 1974 to 2003 for bonds; Keisman, Kelhoffer, and Zennario (2004): S&P, 1988 to 2002; Cantor and Varma (2005): Moody's, 1983 to 2003; Emery and Ou (2009): Moody's, 1990 to 2008 for loans and 1982 to 2008 for bonds.

[4] Recovery rates are confined to the unit interval, assuming that no priority violations between debt and equity holders occur.

Determinants other than seniority and collateral are found to exert influence on recovery rates, as well. For instance, Covitz and Han (2004) and Cantor and Varma (2005) examine the impact of a number of firm- and industry-specific factors. Inter alia, they show that recovery rates are negatively related to firm-specific financial leverage and positively related to firm and industry growth prospects, firm and industry profitability, firm-specific asset tangibility, firm and industry stock returns, and industry capacity utilization. Acharya, Bharath, and Srinivasan (2007) concentrate on the effect of industry health, in particular in conjunction with asset specificity. They show that recovery rates are lower if the issuer's industry is in distress, illiquid or highly leveraged, particularly so if that industry's assets are specific, i.e. of limited use to other industries.

Further, a well-established fact is the strong link between recovery and industry affiliation: Altman and Kishore (1996) and Covitz and Han (2004) find that recovery rates are up to 30 percentage points higher for asset-intense industries such as utilities than for other industries. Hu and Perraudin (2002), Rösch and Scheule (2005) and Cantor and Varma (2005) arrive at similar results. Asset-light industries such as service providers, on the other hand, are generally found to recover less than average.

Other studies analyse the relation to macroeconomic (i.e. systematic) factors: Altman, Brady, Resti, and Sironi (2005), Cantor and Varma (2005), and Chava, Stefanescu, and Turnbull (2008) find that recovery rates are positively related to GDP growth and S&P 500 returns. The same is true for the risk-free rate (Covitz and Han (2004)) and indicators that measure the health of the economy (Rösch and Scheule (2005)). A negative relation, on the other hand, is found for equity volatility (Trück, Harpaintner, and Rachev (2005)) and the level of speculative-grade credit spreads (Cantor and Varma (2005)).

This implies that there is a systematic component in recovery risk that cannot be diversified away. Default arrival risk is known to entail a systematic component as well[5] from which it follows that default and recovery rates must be negatively related. A number of studies present evidence that this is indeed so. For instance, Frye (2000a) finds that recovery rates of bank loans fall about 25 percentage points in years default rates peak. Results of Friedman and Sandow (2003) point in the same direction. Frye (2000b, 2003), Acharya, Bharath, and Srinivasan (2006), and Bruche and Gonzáles-Aguado (2009) show that the effect is disproportionately high for senior, well-collateralized obligations. To see why this is, consider the extreme case of a completely unsecured obligation that recovers zero even in normal times.

[5] See, for instance, Fons (1987), Berndt et al. (2005), Driessen (2005), Saita (2006), and Pan and Singleton (2008).

Clearly, the recovery rate of this obligation cannot worsen further, quite contrary to the one of a well-secured obligation.

Frye (2000b), Hu and Perraudin (2002), Pykhtin (2003), and Rösch and Scheule (2005) show that as a consequence, loss distributions are considerably worse if the negative relation of default and recovery rates is taken into account. Using empirical data, Düllmann and Trapp (2004) estimate that presuming independence results in an underestimation of economic capital by approximately 14 to 17%. Altman, Brady, Resti, and Sironi (2005) even estimate this figure at 30%.

The presence of a systematic component in recovery risk suggests that implied expected recovery rates should be lower than expected future physical realizations, or else investors would not be compensated for bearing this risk. Further, Güntay, Madan, and Unal (2003) and Berd (2005) note that diversifying even the idiosyncratic component is practically unfeasible due to the relative scarcity of default events, possibly further widening the gap between implied and physical figures.

2.2 On the Estimation of Implied Recovery Rates

2.2.1 The Identification Problem

A separate estimation of implied default and recovery rates is complicated by the cash flow characteristics of many credit-risky assets, as mentioned in Section 1.[6] Understanding the nature of this complication is useful for comprehending earlier approaches to estimating implied recovery rates and the path followed in this thesis. To simplify matters, the identification problem is illustrated taking the example of a defaultable zero coupon bond, but results apply to other asset classes, such as CDSs, as well.

The value of such bond at time t, denoted by $V_t(\rho, T)$ and expressed in percent of par, is a function of its discounted expected future cash flows under the risk-neutral measure Q:

$$\frac{V_t(\rho,T)}{M_t} = E_t^Q\left[\frac{1\cdot\left(1-1_{\{\tau\leq T\}}\right)}{M_T} + X(\rho,\tau)1_{\{\tau\leq T\}}exp\left(-\int_t^\tau r_s ds\right)\right] \qquad (2.1)$$

where $M_t = \exp\left(\int_0^t r_s ds\right)$ is the value of a money market investment at time t, r_t is the instantaneous risk-free rate, T is the maturity of the bond, τ is the time of default, $1_{\{\tau\leq T\}}$ is an

[6] A discussion of the identification problem can also be found in Duffee (1998), Duffie (1999), Duffie and Singleton (1999), Christensen (2005), and Houweling and Vorst (2005).

indicator function that equals one if a default has occurred before or in T and zero otherwise, and $X(\rho,\tau)$ is the payment the investor receives if the bond defaults in $\tau \leq T$. The first term on the right hand-side of Eq. (2.1) thus represents the principal payment promised by the bond, paid if the issuer survives, whereas the second term represents the recovery payment, paid if the issuer defaults before or at the maturity date.

To further simplify Eq. (2.1), it is helpful to employ the so-called recovery of treasury convention which assumes that the default-conditional recovery rate, denoted by ρ, is with respect to then-current value of the default-free zero coupon bond with maturity T, denoted by $B_\tau(T)$, such that:

$$X(\rho,\tau) = \rho B_\tau(T) = \rho\, exp\left(-\int_\tau^T r_s ds\right) \tag{2.2}$$

and $X(\rho,T)=\rho$. Because of $exp\left(-\int_t^\tau r_s\, ds\right)\cdot exp\left(-\int_\tau^T r_s ds\right) = \frac{1}{M_T}$, substituting Eq. (2.2) into Eq. (2.1) then allows it to write:

$$\frac{V_t(\rho,T)}{M_t} = E_t^Q\left[\frac{1\cdot\left(1-1_{\{\tau\leq T\}}\right)+\rho 1_{\{\tau\leq T\}}}{M_T}\right] = E_t^Q\left[\frac{1-(1-\rho)1_{\{\tau\leq T\}}}{M_T}\right]. \tag{2.3}$$

In Eq. (2.3), loss given default and the probability of default are multiplicatively linked and many different combinations of both factors result in the same asset price. To produce a practical example, consider the reduced-from framework of Jarrow and Turnbull (1995), Lando (1998), Duffie and Singleton (1999), and others, in which the probability of default under the risk-neutral measure is given by:

$$E^Q\left[1_{\{\tau\leq T\}}\right] = E^Q\left[1-exp\left(-\int_t^T \lambda_s\, ds\right)\right] \tag{2.4}$$

where λ_t is the instantaneous default arrival rate at time t. Substituting Eq. (2.4) into Eq. (2.3), setting λ_t equal to the constant default arrival rate λ^Q and assuming constant interest rates shows that the bond's one-year risk-neutral probability of default, denoted by PD^Q, can be derived as follows:

$$\frac{V_t(\rho,T)}{M_t} = \frac{1-(1-\rho^Q)\left(1-exp\left(-\lambda^Q(T-t)\right)\right)}{M_T}$$

$$\Leftrightarrow 1 - exp\left(-\lambda^Q(T-t)\right) = \frac{1 - \frac{V_t(\rho,T)M_T}{M_t}}{(1-\rho^Q)}$$

$$\Leftrightarrow PD^Q = 1 - exp(-\lambda^Q) = 1 + \left(\frac{1 - \frac{V_t(\rho,T)M_T}{M_t}}{(1-\rho^Q)} - 1\right)^{\frac{1}{T-t}}. \qquad (2.5)$$

Figure 2.2 illustrates that many combinations of loss given default and the probability of default result in the same price of the defaultable discount bond (assumed to be 80% of par): As the recovery rate rises (i.e. loss given default falls), an appropriate increase in the probability of default keeps the bond price constant. Up to a recovery rate of around 60%, this increase is relatively minor but becomes substantial as loss given default approaches zero.[7]

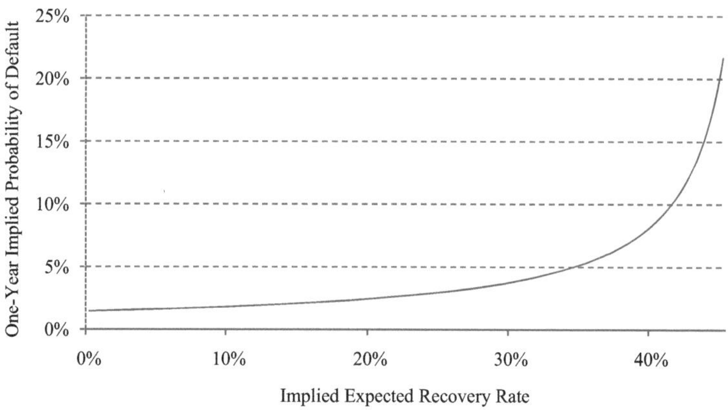

Figure 2.2: Graphical Illustration of the Identification Problem
This figure illustrates that a given price of a defaultable zero coupon bond can result from many different combinations of the implied expected recovery rate and the implied probability of default. The example assumes that the bond's one-year probability of default is given by Eq. (2.5) and that $t = 0$, T= 5, $r_t = 3\%$, and $V_t(\rho, T) = 80\%$.

It is therefore not possible to tell which share of the bond's discount is attributable to the implied probability of default and which share is attributable to the implied recovery rate. In the case of CDSs, the same argument applies with respect to the CDS premium. It follows that implied default and recovery rates cannot be identified separately (i.e. instead of estimating

[7] Houweling and Vorst (2005) arrive at similar results.

solely their product, the implied expected loss) from market prices of these instruments, unless a model setup is chosen that resolves the issue.

2.2.2 A Review of Earlier Studies

The body of literature concerned with the estimation of implied recovery rates has grown considerably over the past decade, and the interest in the topic, undoubtedly fostered by the recent economic developments, is evidenced by a number of articles published of late. All of these have in common that they devise methods to discriminate default and recovery risk in one way or another, and, as noted in the previous section, this undertaking is by no means trivial. Efforts to that effect can be separated into four major strands, and for the purpose of perspicuity, it is practicable to discuss these thematically instead of proceeding in order of publication.

Method 1: Specification of a Link Between Implied Default and Recovery Rates

Bakshi, Madan, and Zhang (2006) show that an empirical separation of implied default and recovery rates is feasible if both are explicitly related to a common state variable: They define the risk-neutral hazard rate λ_t^Q as a function of the risk-free rate r_t, such that $\lambda_t^Q = \vartheta_0 + \vartheta_1 r_t$ and impose a relation to the risk-neutral expected recovery rate ρ_t^Q, such that $\rho_t^Q = \xi_0 + \xi_1 exp(-\lambda_t^Q)$ where ϑ_0, ϑ_1, ξ_0, and ξ_1 are constant parameters. As a result, their model is capable of representing a flexible correlation structure between default, recovery, and interest rates. Employing a simple least-squares approach, they calibrate parameters to prices of 25 BBB-rated, unsecured bonds of major U.S. corporates (data from 1989 to 1998). The average risk-neutral expected recovery rate across all firms and the entire observation period is 48.5%, assuming that recovery of treasury applies. ξ_1 is strictly positive for all firms, suggesting that implied default and recovery rates are negatively related.

In an analogue procedure, Gaspar and Slinko (2008) model hazard and recovery rates as explicit functions of the S&P 500 such that $\partial\lambda_t^Q/\partial S\&P_t < 0$ and $\partial\rho_t^Q/\partial S\&P_t > 0$, i.e. λ_t^Q and ρ_t^Q are negatively related by definition. Further, they assume that the expected risk-neutral recovery rate is identical across all firms. Using Moody's benchmark yields for investment grade U.S. corporate bonds (data from 2004 to 2007), they find that the average firm-wide implied expected recovery rate for these instruments is around 30%.

Das and Hanouna (2009), too, impose an explicit relation between default and recovery risk. Their approach is, however, original in that it allows estimating the entire term structure of implied default and recovery rates, i.e. the recovery rate conditional on survival until a particular future point in time. Also, they evite use of time series data and require as input only the current term structure of CDS premia and information on the issuer's stock. The risk-neutral hazard rate at the jth time step and the ith node of a recombining binomial tree is defined as $\lambda_{i,j}^{Q} = 1/S_{i,j}{}^{\vartheta}$ where $S_{i,j}$ is the stock price at that note and ϑ is a constant parameter. As $S_{i,j}$ approaches infinity (zero), $\lambda_{i,j}^{Q}$ thus approaches zero (infinity). The one-year risk-neutral expected recovery rate is assumed to be related to the hazard rate by $\rho_{i,j}^{Q} = N(\xi_0 + \xi_1 PD_{i,j}^{Q})$, where $PD_{i,j}^{Q} = 1 - exp(-\lambda_{i,j}^{Q})$, $N(\cdot)$ is the cumulative normal distribution, and ξ_0 and ξ_1 are constant parameters. To illustrate the implementation of this method, they divide their universe of 3.130 distinct issuers (data from 2000 to 2002) into five groups with descending credit quality (proxied by expected default frequencies as estimated by CreditMetrics). For each of these groups, they then derive the term structure of CDS premia, to be used in the estimation procedure. Results suggest that, independently of credit quality, the term structure of recovery rates is declining, i.e. expected recovery is higher when the firm defaults sooner rather than later. The authors argue that this may be due to firms drifting slowly into default suffering a greater dissipation of assets than firms defaulting due to a short-term surprise, such as fraud. Further, the level of the forward curve is higher for high-quality firms (around 90%) than for lower-quality firms (30 to 80%). Thus, only for the latter are estimates of implied recovery somewhere close to historically observed figures, the authors supposing that this is because almost all actual default events stem from this group. Finally, across all credit qualities, ξ_1 is negative, implying a reverse relation between default and recovery rates, a result in accordance with Bakshi, Madan, and Zhang (2006).

Method 2: Use of CDS Term Structure Information

A second class of models exploits the fact that premia of long-lived CDSs are particularly sensitive to changes in the implied expected recovery rate, allowing it to separate implied default and recovery rates if the latter are held constant across maturities. Zhang (2003) adopts this approach using Argentinean CDSs with a maturity of one to ten years for the 22 months preceding the country's default in December 2001. He specifies the risk-neutral default arrival rate as a function of two state variables (slope and level of the term structure of the risk-free rate) and supposes that the implied expected recovery rates is constant over time and across maturities. He then calibrates his model to all CDS maturities simultaneously, finding that a global implied expected recovery rate of 27.5% results in the lowest total estimation error. Thus, in contrast to Das and Hanouna (2009), he uses CDS term structure information as a means of separating default and recovery risk and not for the purpose of extracting the term structure of implied recovery rates.

Pan and Singleton (2008) proceed similarly but unlike Zhang (2003), they do not suppose time-invariance. Using term structure information on sovereign CDSs (data from 2001 to 2006), they estimate average risk-neutral expected recovery rates for Mexico, Turkey, and Korea at 76.9, 76.4, and 16.7%, respectively. Considering that it is market convention for the pricing of sovereign CDSs to fix implied expected recovery rates at 25%, these figures seem reasonable only for Korea. The authors re-estimate their model for Mexico and Turkey based on a less turbulent sub-sample (2003 to 2006) and find that results are plausible for Mexico (21.9%) but still somewhat off-market for Turkey (63.3%).

Schneider, Sögner, and Veza (2009) adopt this methodology to CDSs on senior unsecured bonds. Searching for liquidly-traded contracts, they identify 278 large U.S. corporates for which CDS term structure information is available in a sensible quality (data from 2004 to 2008). Analogously to Zhang (2003), they assume implied recovery rates to be constant over time and across maturities, obtaining estimates ranging from 68.7% for firms in the consumer goods sector to 89.9% for utilities, the average over all firms being 79.0%. This conflicts with historically observed recovery rates for senior unsecured bonds, which are, as discussed earlier, more in the range of 40% and thus implicates negative premia for taking recovery risk.

Method 3: Construction of a Default Risk-Free Metric

Madan and Unal (1998) pursue a different concept. They show that the normalized price difference between two credit-risky assets, if both issued by the same firm, is a function only of that firm's capital structure and the default-conditional probability distribution of recovery (i.e. not of default risk) such that the latter can be estimated in a straightforward manner. This, however, assumes implied default and recovery rates to be independent. Supposing further that recovery rates follow a beta distribution with constant mean and constant standard deviation (both, over time and across all firms), they implement their approach using junior and senior certificates of deposit (CDs) of U.S. financial institutions (data from 1987 to 1990). For tractability, they use as inputs the average industry-wide capital structure and average sample-wide CD prices. Their estimates are 36.3% for the implied expected firm-wide recovery rate and 9.9% for the standard deviation. The latter seems quite low, considering that comparable figures for historically realized recovery rates lie more in the range of 20 to 30%. This is likely to be attributable to their using average sample-wide CD prices by which they effectively estimate an industry-wide average recovery rate, in which case the corresponding standard deviation should naturally be lower than for individual firms.

Güntay, Madan, and Unal (2003) apply this proceeding to pairs of junior and senior U.S. corporate bonds (data from 1990 to 1997). Some complications arise from bonds' maturities and coupon structures seldom matching precisely, making necessary adequate adjustment procedures. Issuers' capital structure is proxied by the share of senior debt. It seems, however, questionable whether this is accurate a measure considering that corporate financing draws upon a number of differently-ranked debt instruments.[8] Further, the authors suppose that recovery rates follow a transformed normal distribution with support in the unit interval and model the mean of this distribution as a function of the risk-free rate and firm-specific asset tangibility, holding the standard deviation at a to-be-estimated constant. Allowing for violations of the absolute priority rule (APR)[9], they find that the mean is generally positively related to both, the risk-free rate and the proportion of a firm's tangible assets, with estimates of risk-neutral expected firm-wide recovery rates ranging from 9.6 to 63.3%, depending on the issuer. In all but two cases, these figures are lower than average historical realizations of respective industries which is as one would expect if implied estimates are to carry a risk premium. The standard deviation of firm-wide recovery rates is 6.5% on average with individual estimates coming out as low as 0.9%. This appears rather unrealistic since it suggests that investors can predict the outcome of bankruptcy resolutions with near certainty, in which case they should, however, not require a compensation for taking recovery risk.

Method 4: Separate Estimation of the Implied Probability of Default

Song (2008) tackles the separation problem from the opposite direction: He shows that the premium of a forward CDS commencing in t_1 and terminating in t_2 can be expressed as a function of its premium leg and additionally the premium legs of two spot CDSs, one terminating in t_1, the other terminating in t_2. This is true independently of the processes that govern default arrival and recovery as long as both are assumed to be independent. The respective protection legs (and thus implied expected recovery rates), on the other hand, do not enter the equation such that implied probabilities of default can be estimated uncomplicatedly. In a second step, results are then used to deduce implied recovery rates. Implementing his approach using CDS premia on ten emerging markets sovereigns (data from 1999 to 2005), he finds that implied expected recovery rates are around 25% for most countries, exhibiting very little variation over time. The only exceptions are Brazil and Venezuela for which recovery rates decrease notably in times implied default probabilities spike.

Le (2007) chooses yet another proceeding: First, he extracts firm-specific risk-neutral probabilities of default from equity and call option data using a recombining lattice and assuming that stock prices follow a jump-diffusion process. This presupposes that the APR holds, in which case stock prices will be recovery-insensitive. Similarly to Song (2008), he then uses

8 It is, for instance, not uncommon for corporate issuers to have senior secured, senior unsecured, senior subordinated, and junior subordinated debt outstanding at the same time.

9 According to the APR, claims under a certain liability are satisfied only if all claims that are relatively senior have been satisfied *in full*.

the thusly estimated probabilities of default to calculate risk-neutral expected recovery rates from CDS premia. His data consists of USD-denominated instruments referencing senior unsecured bonds of 1.377 distinct corporate issuers, with observations ranging from 2002 to 2005. In most cases, results lie within the unit interval and are therefore regarded as potentially valid. He finds that implied recovery rates vary considerably with issuers' credit ratings, decreasing from around 85% for A-rated firms to around 20% for CCC/Caa2-rated firms. This extraordinary divergence is quite remarkable, bearing in mind that figures are conditional on default, and hence default proximity should be of limited relevance. In this aspect, results are very similar to those of Das and Hanouna (2009), calling for the conjecture that the strong link between ratings and implied recovery might be an artifact of including equity prices in the estimation procedure. Next, he examines the impact of various firm-specific factors and, consistent with intuition, finds that implied recovery is higher for firms with low financial leverage, low equity volatility, high profitability and a high Q-ratio (market value of debt and equity divided by book value of assets). Implied recovery rates decline from around 60% in mid-2002 to around 45% in mid-2005. During the same time, average implied probabilities of default come down markedly as well, suggesting a positive relation between the two. This is at odds with Bakshi, Madan, and Zhang (2006) and Das and Hanouna (2009), as well as with empirical research discussed earlier, finding a pronounced negative link between physical default and recovery rates (although, strictly speaking, dynamics could be different under the risk-neutral measure).

Table 2.1 gives an overview of the discussion in this section. The methods put forth by Bakshi, Madan, and Zhang (2006), Gaspar and Slinko (2008), and Das and Hanouna (2009) have in common that they define implied default and recovery rates as functions of one (or more) state variable(s) such that a simultaneous identification is feasible. This, however, comes at the severe disadvantage of estimation results being impacted importantly by model specifications. It is, for instance, not a priory evident why default and recovery should be a function only of the risk-free rate (Bakshi, Madan, and Zhang) nor does an imposed negative relation between the two (Gaspar and Slinko) promise unprejudiced estimates.

Zhang (2003), Pan and Singleton (2008), and Schneider, Sögner, and Veza (2009) avoid this shortcoming by employing the entire term structure of CDS premia to separately identify implied recovery rates. As CDS trading concentrates mostly on the five year maturity, the applicability of this procedure is, however, constrained to highly liquid contracts, such as CDSs on sovereigns or major corporates. Further, their proceeding necessitates the assumption that implied recovery rates are constant across maturities. This conflicts with results of Das and Hanouna (2009) who find that the term structure of forward recovery rates is downward-sloping, particularly for lower-quality firms.[10] Further, only Zhang arrives at economically meaningful results (Pan and Singleton only for Korea), and he assumes that recovery rates are constant over time.

Madan and Unal (1998), Güntay, Madan, and Unal (2003), Le (2007), and Song (2008) derive equations that are entirely free of either default or recovery risk. In the first case, this is achieved by relating the priority of junior and senior debt holders' claims to simplistic proxies of issuers' capital structure. This allows it to estimate the entire implied probability distribution of recovery given default, provided that the functional form of this distribution is specified (Madan and Unal assume a beta distribution, Güntay, Madan, and Unal a transformed normal distribution). This is very different from all other approaches which only model the implied expected recovery rate (i.e. the mean of an unknown distribution).[11] In the second case (Le, Song), implied probabilities of default are estimated from equity/equity option data and premia of spot and forward CDSs, respectively, and are then used to calculate implied recovery rates. In all four models it is assumed that implied default and recovery rates are independent, or else a separation would not be feasible.

In summary, prior approaches to estimating implied recovery suppose either i) constant implied recovery rates (over time, over firms, or both), ii) an explicit relation to the implied probability of default or iii) independence between the two. It is questionable whether these assumptions do justice to the true characteristics of implied recovery rates, and estimation results, even if economically meaningful, should therefore be treated cautiously.

---

[10] For the lowest-quality firms in their sample, Das and Hanouna estimate the one-year risk-neutral recovery rate at 80%, declining monotonously to 30% for the five year maturity.

[11] Gaspar and Slinko (2008) suppose, too, that implied recovery rates follow a beta distribution but essentially model only the mean of this distribution.

	Bakshi, Madan, and Zhang (2006)	Gaspar and Slinko (2008)	Das and Hanouna (2009)	Zhang (2003)	Pan and Singleton (2008)
General Approach	Specification of explicit link between λ^Q and ρ^Q	Specification of explicit link between λ^Q and ρ^Q	Specification of explicit link between λ^Q and ρ^Q	Calibration over several CDS maturities simultaneously	Use of divergent sensitiv. of long and short-lived CDSs to changes in ρ^Q
Major Assumptions	λ^Q and ρ^Q are functions of the risk-free rate	λ^Q and ρ^Q are neg. rel. and func. of the S&P. ρ^Q const. across firms	λ^Q and ρ^Q are functions of the issuer's stock price and stock volatility	Constant ρ^Q, both over time and across CDS maturities	Constant ρ^Q across CDS maturities
Data	25 BBB-rated, unsecured U.S. corporate bonds, 1989 to 1998	Moody's benchm. yields for Aaa and Baa U.S. corp. bonds, 2004 to 07	CDS term structure data for CDSs on 3,130 corp. issuers, 2000 to 2002	CDS term structure data for Argentina, 2000 to 2001	CDS term structure data for Mexico, Turkey, and Korea, 2001 to 2006
Results	Avg. unsecured ρ^Q under recovery of treasury: 48.5%. Neg. rel. between λ^Q and ρ^Q	Avg. firm-wide ρ^Q: ~ 30%	Avg. ρ^Q betw. ~ 90% for high-qual. firms to ~ 30 - 80% for low-qual. firms. Neg. rel. betw. λ^Q and ρ^Q	Avg. ρ^Q: 27.5%	Avg. ρ^Q: 76.9% for Mexico, 76.4% for Turkey, 16.7% for Korea

	Schneider, Sögner, and Veza (2009)	Madan and Unal (1998)	Güntay, Madan, and Unal (2003)	Le (2007)	Song (2008)
General Approach	Use of divergent sensitiv. of long and short-lived CDSs to changes in ρ^Q	Construction of a default risk-free metric using jun. and sen. debt	Construction of a default risk-free metric using jun. and sen. debt	Estim. of λ^Q from stocks and calls, then calc. of ρ^Q from CDS premia	Construction of a rec. risk-free metric using spot and forw. CDSs
Major Assumptions	Constant ρ^Q, both over time and across CDS maturities	λ^Q and ρ^Q are indep., ρ^Q is beta-distrib. with const. mean and st. dev. over time and firms	λ^Q and ρ^Q are indep., ρ^Q follows a transf. normal distrib. with constant standard deviation	λ^Q and ρ^Q are independent	λ^Q and ρ^Q are independent
Data	CDS term structure data for 278 U.S. corporates, 2004 to 2008	Junior and senior CDs of U.S. financial institutions, 1987 to 1990	Junior and senior bonds of 28 U.S. corporates, 1990 to 1997	Senior unsec., USD-denom. CDSs on 1.377 corp. issuers, 2002 to 05	Spot and forward CDSs on ten emerging markets sovereigns, 1999 to 2005
Results	ρ^Q ranging from 68.7% for consumer goods to 89.9% for utilities	Avg. firm-wide ρ^Q: 36.3%, avg. standard deviation of ρ^Q: 9.9%	Avg. firm-wide ρ^Q: 31.2%, avg. st. dev. of ρ^Q: 6.5%. Mostly $\rho^Q < \rho^P$	Avg. sen. unsec. ρ^Q from 20% to 85% (A to CCC). Pos. rel. betw. λ^Q and ρ^Q	Avg. ρ^Q: ~ 25% for most countries. Little time-var. of ρ^Q or neg. rel. to λ^Q

Table 2.1: Prior Literature on the Estimation of Implied Recovery Rates

This table shows an overview of prior literature concerned with the estimation of implied recovery rates from credit-risky assets.

3 A New Approach to Estimating Market-Implied Recovery Rates

This chapter illustrates generically how implied recovery rates can be extracted from CDS premia and capital structure information:[12] Section 3.1 first shows that the (observable) ratio of premia of two CDSs referencing the same firm but different types of debt of this firm is a function only of respective implied expected recovery rates but not of the implied probability of default. Section 3.2 then illustrates how this ratio can be expressed as a function of capital structure information if a functional form for the implied probability distribution of recovery is supposed. Section 3.3 discusses sensible characteristics of the latter and chooses a beta distribution for the further proceeding.

3.1 A Default-Free Metric of Implied Recovery

CDSs allow trading the credit risk associated with a certain debt instrument (reference obligation), issued by some firm or sovereign (reference entity). If the reference entity defaults, the CDS seller compensates the CDS buyer for the loss in value of the reference obligation. In return, the CDS buyer pays a periodic premium to the CDS seller until a default occurs or the life of the CDS ends, whichever is earlier. The payments made by the CDS seller and buyer constitute the "protection leg" and the "premium leg", respectively. At inception of the CDS, the premium is commonly chosen such that the value of both legs is identical.

The value of the premium leg at time t, denoted by $P_t(s,T)$, can be expressed as the product of the CDS premium, denoted by s, and the price of an annuity $A_t(T)$ paying one until the reference entity defaults in τ or the CDS expires in T, whichever happens first:

$$P_t(s,T) = sA_t(T). \tag{3.1}$$

Note that in this equation s has no time index because, once fixed at the inception of the transaction, it remains unchanged throughout the life of the CDS.

At maturity, the value of the protection leg, denoted by $PR_T(\rho,T)$, is equal to one minus the recovery rate if the reference entity has defaulted (i.e. equal to the loss given default) and zero otherwise:

[12] The empirical implementation, tailored to the data at hand, is outlined in Chapter 5.

$$PR_T(\rho,T) = (1-\rho)1_{\{\tau\leq T\}} \tag{3.2}$$

where, continuing the notation from Section 2.2.1, ρ is the reference obligation's default-conditional recovery rate at time T, assuming that recovery of treasury applies[13], and $1_{\{\tau\leq T\}}$ is an indicator function that equals one if a default has occurred before or in T and zero otherwise.

Let M_t denote again the value of a money market investment. The normalized process $PR_t(\rho,T)/M_t$ is then a martingale under the risk-neutral measure Q:

$$\frac{PR_t(\rho,T)}{M_t} = E_t^Q\left[\frac{(1-\rho)1_{\{\tau\leq T\}}}{M_T}\right]. \tag{3.3}$$

If the risk-free interest rate is stochastic, then M_T is a random variable and possibly not independent from the numerator in the expectation term such that Eq. (3.3) cannot be simplified further. Changing the numéraire to the default-free zero coupon bond with maturity T, denoted by $B_t(T)$, resolves this issue: The normalized process $PR_t(\rho,T)/B_t(T)$ is a martingale under the T-forward measure $\tilde{Q}$:

$$\frac{PR_t(\rho,T)}{B_t(T)} = E_t^{\tilde{Q}}\left[\frac{(1-\rho)1_{\{\tau\leq T\}}}{B_T(T)}\right], \tag{3.4}$$

and because of $B_T(T) = 1$, Eq. (3.4) simplifies to:

$$PR_t(\rho,T) = E_t^{\tilde{Q}}\left[(1-\rho)1_{\{\tau\leq T\}}\right]B_t(T). \tag{3.5}$$

Rearranging the right hand-side of Eq. (3.5) shows that the value of the protection leg is equal to the product of the expected loss given default, the probability of default, and the current price of the risk-free zero coupon bond:

$$\begin{aligned} PR_t(\rho,T) = {} & E_t^{\tilde{Q}}\left[(1-\rho)1_{\{\tau\leq T\}} \middle| 1_{\{\tau\leq T\}} = 1\right]\tilde{Q}_t\left(1_{\{\tau\leq T\}} = 1\right)B_t(T) \\ & + E_t^{\tilde{Q}}\left[(1-\rho)1_{\{\tau\leq T\}} \middle| 1_{\{\tau\leq T\}} = 0\right]\tilde{Q}_t\left(1_{\{\tau\leq T\}} = 0\right)B_t(T) \end{aligned} \tag{3.6}$$

[13] Bakshi, Madan, and Zhang (2006) test several recovery assumptions and find that recovery of treasury indeed matches market prices best. However, Guha (2003) observes that defaulted bonds of the same issuer and the same seniority mostly trade at very similar prices regardless of maturities and finds that only recovery of face value can explain this pattern satisfactorily.

$$= \left(1 - E_t^{\tilde{Q}}\left[\rho \mid 1_{\{\tau \leq T\}} = 1\right]\right) \tilde{Q}_t\left(1_{\{\tau \leq T\}} = 1\right) B_t(T).$$

To set the value of both legs identical, s must be chosen such that:

$$s = \frac{PR_t(\rho, T)}{A_t(T)} = \frac{\left(1 - E_t^{\tilde{Q}}\left[\rho \mid 1_{\{\tau \leq T\}} = 1\right]\right) \tilde{Q}_t\left(1_{\{\tau \leq T\}} = 1\right) B_t(T)}{A_t(T)}. \tag{3.7}$$

Assume two distinct CDSs, both having identical maturities, premium payment dates, and credit event definitions and both referencing the same firm but obligations with different seniorities of that firm. In such a setting, both have different default-conditional recovery rates but identical probabilities of default. Further, let s_{sr} and s_{jr} denote the premium of the CDS referencing the relatively senior and relatively junior obligation, respectively. From Eq. (3.7) it then follows that the ratio s_{sr}/s_{jr}, denoted by R, is solely a function of the recovery rates of these obligations, denoted by ρ_{sr} and ρ_{jr}, and implied expectations at time t:

$$R = \frac{s_{sr}}{s_{jr}} = \frac{1 - E_t^{\tilde{Q}}\left[\rho_{sr} \mid 1_{\{\tau \leq T\}} = 1\right]}{1 - E_t^{\tilde{Q}}\left[\rho_{jr} \mid 1_{\{\tau \leq T\}} = 1\right]}. \tag{3.8}$$

Eq. (3.8) thus isolates implied recovery risk from implied default risk without assuming independence between the two. Note that this simplification is achievable only due to two special characteristics of the cash flow structure in CDSs: First, the payoff under the protection leg occurs only in the event of default but not otherwise, such that all the terms in the numerator of Eq. (3.7) are multiplicatively linked. Second, the payoff under the premium leg is a function only of the implied probability of default but not of the recovery rate such that denominators are identical for both CDSs.

3.2 The Link to Capital Structure

In a default, the firm-wide recovery rate is solely a function of the ratio of firm value to liabilities at default, denoted by x. Assuming that x lies between zero and $e \geq 100\%$, i.e. $x \in]0, e[$ and that debt holders cannot recover more than 100%, the firm-wide recovery rate, denoted by ρ_{firm}, is simply:

$$\rho_{firm}(x) = \begin{cases} x & x \in]0,1] \\ 1 & x \in]1,e[\end{cases} \tag{3.9}$$

According to the APR, claims under a certain liability are satisfied only if all claims that are relatively senior have been satisfied *in full.*[14] Instrument specific recovery rates are thus additionally a function of the issuer's capital structure at the time of default. Let $instr$ denote the percentage that a debt instrument of a particular seniority constitutes of a borrower's total liabilities and further let $instr^-$ and $instr^+$ denote the percentage of liabilities that are relatively junior and senior, respectively, such that $instr^- + instr + instr^+ = 100\%$. The recovery rate at default of such an instrument, denoted by ρ_{instr}, is then given by:

$$\rho_{instr}(x) = \begin{cases} 0 & x \in]0, instr^+] \\ \dfrac{x - instr^+}{instr} & x \in]instr^+, 1 - instr^-] \\ 1 & x \in]1 - instr^-, e[\end{cases} \tag{3.10}$$

Figure 3.1 illustrates Eqs. (3.9) and (3.10), assuming that a debt instrument of a particular seniority accounts for 50% of a borrower's total liabilities, with 30% of liabilities ranking relatively senior (i.e. $instr^+ = 30\%$) and the remainder ranking relatively junior (i.e. $instr^- = 20\%$). If $0 < x \leq instr^+ = 30\%$, holders of this instrument recover nothing, if $instr^+ < x < 1 - instr^- = 80\%$, they recovery only a fraction and if $1 - instr^- \leq x$ they recover 100%. The firm-wide recovery rate is equal to x but does not exceed 100%.

For any given implied probability density function of recovery given default $h_t(x)$, implied expected recovery rates and the variance of implied recovery rates at time t are given by:

$$E_t^{\tilde{Q}}[\rho \,|1_{\{\tau \leq T\}} = 1] = \int_0^e \rho(x) h_t(x) dx, \tag{3.11}$$

$$Var_t^{\tilde{Q}}[\rho \,|1_{\{\tau \leq T\}} = 1] = \int_0^e \left(\rho(x) - \int_0^e \rho(x) h_t(x) dx,\right)^2 h_t(x) dx. \tag{3.12}$$

[14] Deviations from absolute priority of debt claims over equity claims have become very rare for publicly traded firms (see Baird, Bris, and Zhu (2007) and Bharath and Panchapegesan (2007)). APR violations within different types of debt are however less well-researched.

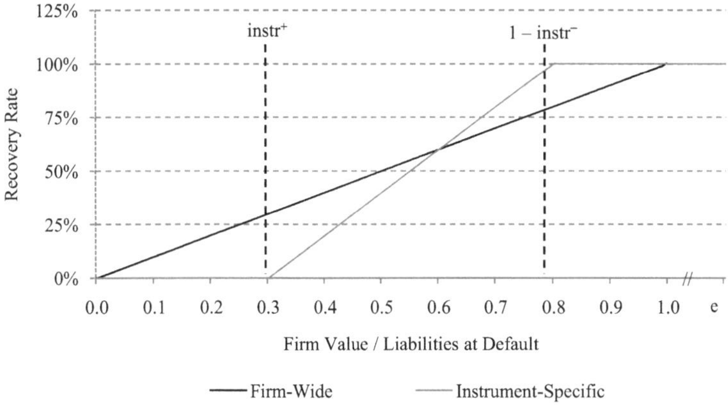

Figure 3.1: Illustrative Recovery Rates Given Default (I)
This figure illustrates the relationships between the ratio of firm value to liabilities at default and recovery rates for the entire firm and for a debt instrument of a particular seniority. It is assumed that this instrument accounts for 50% of a borrower's total liabilities with 30% of liabilities ranking relatively senior and the remainder ranking relatively junior. Further, it is assumed that the APR holds. Results are obtained using Eqs. (3.9) and (3.10).

Substituting Eqs. (3.10) and (3.11) into Eq. (3.8) permits expressing the model-implied ratio of premia s_{sr}/s_{jr}, denoted by $\bar{R}$, as a functions of the borrower's capital structure and $h_t(x)$:

$$\bar{R} = \frac{s_{sr}}{s_{jr}} = \frac{1 - \int_{sr^+}^{1-sr^-} \frac{x - sr^+}{sr} h_t(x)dx - \int_{1-sr^-}^{e} h_t(x)dx}{1 - \int_{jr^+}^{1-jr^-} \frac{x - jr^+}{jr} h_t(x)dx - \int_{1-jr^-}^{e} h_t(x)dx}. \tag{3.13}$$

By calibrating model-implied ratios $\bar{R}$ to actual ratios R, $h_t(x)$ can be estimated. To this end, a parametric approach is pursued which makes it necessary to specify the functional form of $h_t(x)$. Therefore, it is examined next what requirements such a specification should fulfill.

3.3 The Implied Probability Distribution of Recovery

By definition, recovery rates are strictly non-negative and cannot assume arbitrarily high values. Based on Moody's Ultimate Recovery Database, Cantor, Emery, and Stumpp (2006) and Emery (2007) find that historical realizations of the ratio of firm value to liabilities at default lie mostly between zero and 100% with very few observations reaching values as high as

120%. Ratios above 100% can occur if a firm chooses to strategically default, for instance to obtain relief from lenders and regulators. In such a case, debt holders recover 100% with equity holders receiving the remainder. As these instances are, however, quite rare, it is assumed that x has support in the unit interval and required that $\int_0^1 h_t(x)dx = 1$. At default, the firm-wide recovery rate is then equal to the ratio of firm value to liabilities at default, i.e. $\rho_{firm} = x,\ x \in]0,1[$, and it follows that the expected firm-wide recovery rate is equal to the mean of $h_t(x)$, i.e.:

$$E_t^{\tilde{Q}}\left[\rho_{firm} | 1_{\{\tau \leq T\}} = 1\right] = \int_0^1 x h_t(x)dx. \tag{3.14}$$

The same is true with respect to the variance, i.e.:

$$Var_t^{\tilde{Q}}\left[\rho_{firm} | 1_{\{\tau \leq T\}} = 1\right] = \int_0^1 \left(x - \int_0^1 x h_t(x)dx\right)^2 h_t(x)dx. \tag{3.15}$$

Following the approach of Madan and Unal (1998), Gaspar and Slinko (2008), and rating agencies such as Moody's (see Gupton and Stein (2002) and Cantor, Emery, and Stumpp (2006)), recovery rates are modeled using a beta distribution. Beta distributions are bounded on both sides, can assume a variety of shapes and are fully specified by their first two moments. Assuming the lower and upper bound to be zero and unity, respectively, the density function of the beta distribution at time t is given by:

$$bet_t(x) = \frac{x^{p_t-1}(1-x)^{q_t-1}}{\int_0^1 y^{p_t-1}(1-y)^{q_t-1}dy} \quad p_t, q_t \in]0,\infty[\tag{3.16}$$

where p_t and q_t are shape parameters.

As shown in Appendix A.I, the supremum and infimum of the standard deviation of the beta distribution for a given mean are:

$$\sigma_{sup,t} = \sqrt{\mu_t - {\mu_t}^2} \quad \mu_t \in]0,1[, \tag{3.17}$$

$$\sigma_{inf} = 0. \tag{3.18}$$

The first two moments of the beta distribution are thus related: As the mean approaches zero or unity, the standard deviation approaches zero. The highest possible standard deviation is 50% and requires that $\mu = 50\%$. For relatively small standard deviations, distributions are approximately bell-shaped. As the standard deviation increases, probability masses concentrate on either side and distributions eventually assume a U-shape. In this case, realizations of x close to zero or unity are more likely than realizations in between and probability densities approach infinity at endpoints. Figure 3.2 illustrates this for $\mu = 50\%$.

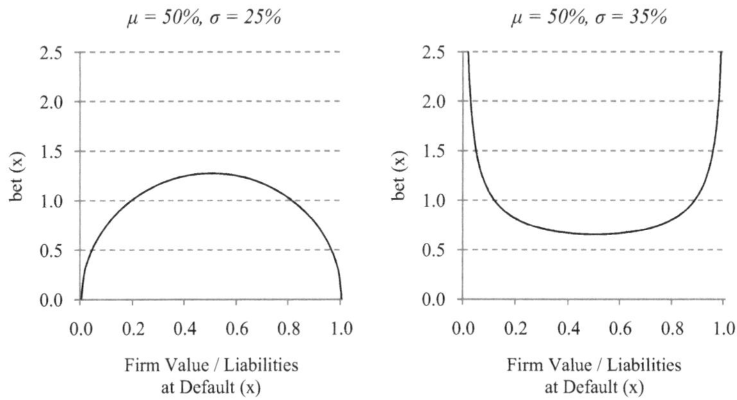

Figure 3.2: Illustrative Densities of the Beta Distribution
This figure illustrates exemplary probability densities of a beta distribution with support in the unit interval, assuming $\mu = 50\%$, $\sigma = 25\%$ (left chart) and $\mu = 50\%$, $\sigma = 35\%$ (right chart). Results are obtained using Eq. (3.16).

4 A Review of Appropriable Credit Derivatives

The approach pursued in this thesis requires pairs of CDSs referencing differently-ranked debt of a single issuer, as the previous chapter showed. To the end of identifying suitable combinations, Section 4.1 provides an overview of debt instruments typically employed by non-sovereign issuers to fulfill their financing needs, and briefly describes the different types of CDSs outstanding thereon. The discussion reveals that workable combinations will consist either of two CDSs referencing differently-ranked bonds or of a CDS referencing a high-yield bond and an LCDS referencing a leveraged loan. In the former case, a combination is straightforward as CDS transactions are commonly concluded based on broadly accepted standard terms which are identical irrespective of the underlyings' seniority. In the latter case, however, complications arise from several fundamental particularities of LCDSs, and a diligent assessment of this matter is required. For that purpose, Section 4.2 reviews the key characteristics of leveraged loans and bonds, thus preparing the ground for Section 4.3, in which the properties of CDSs and LCDSs are compared in greater detail. Section 4.4 then attempts to quantify the effect of divergent provisions and evaluates the usability of U.S. and European LCDSs, respectively, for the purpose of this thesis.

4.1 Credit Default Swaps on Corporate Debt

To raise debt, companies may issue bonds or loans[15], both of which are associated with a certain seniority or ranking. In a credit event, the borrower's remaining assets are distributed according to the waterfall principle: Obligations with the highest seniority are repaid first, and only if assets remain thereafter are obligations with lower seniorities repaid. Further, debt instruments may be secured or unsecured: If certain of the borrower's assets are ring-fenced to serve as collateral for the lenders under a particular obligation only, this obligation is called "secured". Together, seniority and collateral determine the *priority* of an obligation

Most bonds are either senior secured, senior unsecured, senior subordinated, or junior subordinated whereas loans are either senior secured or senior unsecured. Loans issued by sub-investment grade firms are mostly senior secured and rank higher than all other debt of the

[15] As well as other debt-like instruments not discussed here.

borrower.[16] Commonly, these loans are funded by a syndicate of lending banks and are accordingly also referred to as "syndicated secured loans". Loans issued by investment grade firms, on the other hand, are mostly senior unsecured and rank pari passu to senior unsecured bonds of the borrower.

A bond is called "high-yield" if it is rated sub-investment grade, i.e. BB+ or lower according to the rating methodologies of Fitch and S&P and Ba1 or lower according to that of Moody's. In practice, most bonds of sub-investment grade issuers have a sub-investment grade rating and are thus high yield. Similarly, a loan is called "leveraged" if it is rated sub-investment grade and/or its spread above the risk-free rate or the borrower's debt/EBITDA ratio exceeds a certain level. S&P, for instance, calls a loan "leveraged" if it is rated sub-investment grade or if it is rated investment grade but pays interest of at least LIBOR + 125 basis points (BPs).[17] Bloomberg uses a hurdle rate of LIBOR + 250 BPs.[18] Most loans of sub-investment grade issuers fulfill these criteria and qualify as leveraged loans. In this thesis, the terms "leveraged loan" and "syndicated secured loan" are therefore used interchangeably.

Reference obligations in CDSs may be bonds of all priorities as well as senior unsecured loans. CDSs are, however, not intended to reference leveraged loans because CDS do not, as will be argued in Sections 4.2 and 4.3, adequately account for the "secured" feature and other characteristics of these loans. Credit derivatives on this asset class were therefore generally not available up until a few years ago, or only on a bespoke[19] basis.

This is particularly noteworthy if one considers that leveraged loans, and not high-yield bonds, constitute the primary funding source of sub-investment grade borrowers, as Figure 4.1 illustrates. Between 2003 and 2009, leveraged loans accounted for more than three quarters of the total new financing of these firms, both in the U.S. and in Europe, and with few exceptions this share increased over time. In 2006 and 2007, the loan issuance volume was in excess of USD 600bn in the U.S. and EUR 200bn in Europe. The breakout of the crisis in mid-2007, however, brought these figures down to below 2003 levels as risk aversion increased and the credit market dried up. Since then, volumes have not improved by much (the U.S. market even saw a significant further decline), a development attributable to the lasting weakening of the loan investor base (e.g. banks) and continuing de-leveraging efforts. Issuance volumes of high-yield bonds fell sharply in 2008, too (strikingly, the European high-

16 Conversations with practitioners suggest that senior secured loans in most cases also rank higher than senior secured bonds of the same borrower. However, inter-creditor agreements may stipulate aberrant provisions.

17 See Chew and Miller (2007).

18 See Chamblee and Tenholder (2005).

19 In a bespoke transaction, parties negotiate individual terms and conditions, i.e. they do not necessarily rely on any or all of the relevant standard documentation.

yield market did not see a single transaction) but proved more resilient in 2009 when volumes roughly returned to pre-crisis levels.

LCDSs complement "traditional" CDSs in that they are designed for use with leveraged loans, as opposed to bonds or senior unsecured loans. They are a later development of the market for over-the-counter (OTC) credit derivatives: In June 2006, the International Swaps and Derivatives Organization (ISDA) published standard documentation for single-name U.S. LCDSs. An updated version of this documentation became available in May 2007. In July 2007, ISDA published standard documentation for single-name European LCDSs which was updated in March 2008. While LCDSs had been traded on a bespoke basis before, such documentation spurred the evolution of the LCDS market and proved to be similarly important as comparable standard language was for the CDS market.[20]

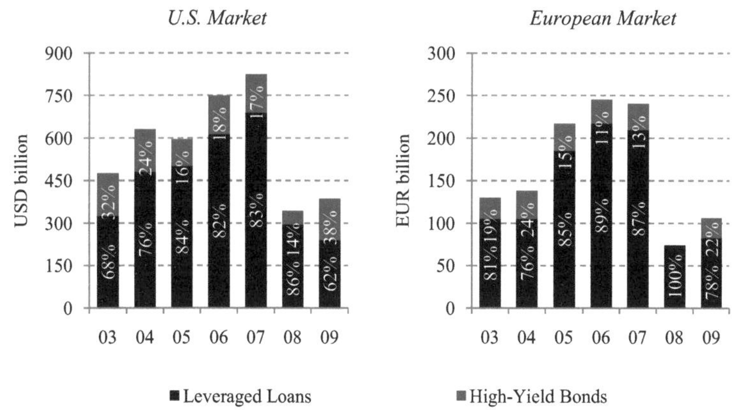

Figure 4.1: Leveraged Loan and High-Yield Bond Issuance Volumes
This figure illustrates issuance volumes of leveraged loans and high-yield bonds for U.S. and European sub-investment grade borrowers between 2003 and 2009. U.S. figures are taken from Loan Pricing Corporation (http://www.loanpricing.com) and European figures are taken from European High Yield Association (http://www.ehya.com).

The benefits of LCDSs are in many ways analogous to those of CDSs. Direct access to syndicated secured loan issuances via the primary market is, by definition, a privilege of syndicate members. Also, secondary market trading of these loans often is still thin, despite having developed strongly prior to the sub-prime crisis. LCDSs provide the opportunity to build exposure to this asset class in an efficient, tax- and cost-saving manner without use of the cash

[20] See Duncan (2006).

market. Further, they are of particular interest to those who cannot participate directly in syndicated lending due to regulatory restrictions and banking monopoly laws.

Syndicate members, on the other hand, are interested in shifting credit risk from their balance sheets, particularly in light of the regulatory standards set forth by Basel II. These require banks, among other things, to match their credit risk by a certain amount of own equity, depending on the degree of that instrument's risk. This "risk weighting" is particularly high for leveraged loans, tying up banks' equity. With credit protection in place (i.e. through a purchase of LCDSs), banks can hedge their positions and thus reduce risk weightings without actually having to sell their loans. This benefits client relationships and is particularly advantageous if secondary market trading is illiquid. Further, LCDSs enable investors to pursue trading strategies that require short exposure to leveraged loans. Shorting loans is generally not possible in the cash market, but investors can synthesize such positions by entering into an LCDS as protection buyer.

CDSs are for the most part concluded based on commonly accepted standard language and are therefore identically structured. In the sense of Eq. (3.8), the ratio of two CDSs referencing the same issuer should thus be a function of implied expected recovery rates only, provided that maturities and credit event definitions match. Unfortunately, the same is not necessarily true for combinations of LCDSs and CDSs: While standard language for LCDSs is in many ways similar to that of CDSs, it, however, includes several additional provisions to account for the specifics of leveraged loans. This implies that LCDS and CDS pricing formulas might diverge in which case Eq. (3.8) would no longer be an uncontaminated measure of implied recovery. In order to appreciate the ensuing implications for the approach pursued in this thesis, a thorough understanding of leveraged loans and bonds is required to begin with.

4.2 Leveraged Loans and Bonds

Leveraged loans provide borrowers with a vehicle to raise funds from a limited universe of financing banks, whereas bonds are typically marketed to a broader investor base. This has important implications with regard to origination processes, disclosure requirements, and transferability. Further, the sub-investment grade status of leveraged loan issuers and the natural desire of lenders to limit their credit risk exposures greatly influence how topics such as collateral, covenants, coupons, and prepayment are handled. This section is concerned with a comparison of the structural differences between leveraged loans and bonds. Unless noted otherwise, the factual information presented herein stems from discussions with, and material provided by, the Leveraged Finance Group of a major investment bank.

4.2.1 Origination, Information, and Transferability

Leveraged loans may be arranged either between a borrower and a single lending bank, or, more commonly, between a borrower and a syndicate of lending banks. In the latter case, one (or more) of the lending banks acts as lead arranger. The lead arranger conducts detailed due diligence on the borrower and negotiates basic transaction terms such as the size of the loan, the interest rate, fees, loan structure, covenants and type of syndication. These terms are documented in a "loan agreement". Based on the information received in the due diligence process, the lead arranger prepares the "information memorandum", also called "bank book" which is used to market the transaction to other potential lending banks or institutional investors. Together, the lead arranger and the other lenders constitute the primary market. If the transaction is an "underwritten syndication", the lead arranger guarantees the borrower that the loan's full notional will be placed at a predefined price. If the loan is undersubscribed at that price, he is forced to absorb the difference. If the transaction is a "best-efforts syndication", the lead arranger tries to place the loan at the predefined terms but may, if investor demand is insufficient, adjust these terms to achieve full placement. Alternatively, he may cancel the transaction. In recent years, it has become market custom to use "market-flex language" which allows the lead arranger to adjust the pricing of the loan to steer investor demand. Market-flex language has made best-efforts syndications the rule.

The information memorandum typically includes historical as well as forward-looking financials of the borrower, an industry overview, and the terms and conditions of the transaction. Its precise form is at the discretion of the lead arranger. Some of its content, such as forward-looking financials, will be private information not available in the public domain. Loans are therefore *private debt instruments* and the information transmitted between borrower and lending syndicate is considered confidential. Further, syndicate members often need the borrower's consent if they want to sell their investment to an outside party. Together with the private information issue, these transfer provisions can hamper secondary market trading considerably.

The origination process for bonds is organized by a lead arranger and a group of dealers. The transaction terms agreed between lead arranger/dealers and the borrower are set out in the "bond indenture". Based on the information received in the due diligence process, the lead arranger prepares a "prospectus". An advanced draft of this document, commonly referred to as "red herring", is used to market the bond to investors. The lead arranger or any of the dealers may invest in the bond as initial purchasers. At the issuance stage, they act as underwriters or as placement agents. If they act as underwriters, they are obliged to purchase all those bonds which could not be placed with investors. If they act as placement agents, they are obliged to use best efforts to place the issue but have no obligation to achieve full placement. If the lead arranger/dealers have acquired bonds in the primary market, they may either hold on to these or sell them in the secondary market.

The prospectus in public bond offerings is subject to rigid regulatory disclosure requirements. Therefore, public bond origination can be conducted less quickly and discreetly than (private) leveraged loan issuance. However, the prospectus typically lacks forward-looking financials and other information that is not available in the public domain. Exchange-listed bonds are therefore *public debt instruments* and can be traded much more easily than leveraged loans.[21]

4.2.2 The Structure of Leveraged Loans

Leveraged loans typically consist of a revolving credit facility or "revolver" and of "term loans". Term loans are usually tranched into an amortizing term loan (term loan A), provided by syndicate members, and institutional tranches (term loans B, C and D), provided by institutional investors. In the U.S., amortizing term loans have become increasingly rare as institutional investors are now the primary buyers of leveraged loans. The term loan D, called "second lien tranche", is subordinated to term loans A, B and C, called "first lien tranches", but ranks senior to all other debt of the borrower.[22]

		Lien	Lender	Repayment
Revolving Credit Facility		First lien	Syndicate members	Discretionary
Term Loans	A	First lien	Syndicate members	Amortizing
	B	First lien	Institutional investors	Bullet
	C	First lien	Institutional investors	Bullet
	D	Second lien	Institutional investors	Bullet

Table 4.1: The Typical Structure of Leveraged Loans
This table shows liens, lenders, and prepayment provisions as typically applicable to revolving credit facilities and term loans A to D.

The term loan A is usually repaid on scheduled repayment dates during its life, whereas term loans B, C and D are mostly subject to bullet repayment, i.e. a one-off repayment on the maturity date. Once repaid, term loans cannot be re-borrowed. This is the principal difference to the revolving credit facility, usually provided by syndicate members, which allows the borrower to borrow, repay, and re-borrow funds during the life of the loan in accordance with

21 Not all bonds are exchange-listed. Unlisted bonds are private debt instruments and may be more difficult to trade.

22 Sometimes, even third lien tranches which are subordinated to second lien tranches but senior to all other debt of the borrower, are used.

predetermined conditions. In addition to interest on borrowed funds, borrowers are charged a commitment fee on unused funds. Revolvers are often used to fund working capital and capital expenditure requirements which can fluctuate significantly over time. Table 4.1 summarizes above discussion.

4.2.3 Collateral and Covenants

Leveraged loans are usually secured by particular assets of the borrower, as specified in the loan agreement. In the event of default, lenders can take possession of these assets, liquidate them and use the proceeds to satisfy their claims before any claims of unsecured lenders are redeemed. Bonds, on the other hand, are mostly unsecured and lenders' claims are satisfied out of the other, general assets of the borrower, available for distribution to all debt holders ahead of equity holders. If these assets are not sufficient to repay all of the borrower's obligations, repayment of claims will be apportioned.

Loan agreements and bond indentures usually list a series of covenants that set certain limits within which borrowers must operate their business. Generally speaking, covenants are intended to prevent borrowers from taking action that comes at the expense of lenders, such as further increasing financial leverage. Also, they provide an early warning if the borrower's credit condition deteriorates and allow lenders to take pre-emptive measures. Lenders usually check adherence to covenants on a quarterly basis. In the worst case, a covenant breach can trigger a technical default and the loan or bond becomes due and payable immediately. Several studies show that tight covenants indeed provide a meaningful protection of enterprise value and ultimately lead to higher recovery rates on defaulted obligations.[23] Generally, covenant packages tend to be more comprehensive for lower-rated borrowers.

Several types of covenants exist. Affirmative covenants, which are mostly boilerplate, require the lender to take certain action, such as paying interest in a timely manner. Negative covenants, on the other hand, *prohibit* the lender from taking certain action, such as selling assets, issuing further debt that ranks senior or pari passu, or pursuing major acquisitions. Financial covenants stipulate certain risk measures or performance metrics that the borrower must not exceed or has to achieve, respectively. Of these, five major types exist: Coverage covenants specify a certain minimum ratio of cash flow or earnings to expenses, interest or other charges. Leverage covenants specify a maximum ratio of debt to equity or cash flow. Current-ratio covenants specify a minimum ratio of current assets to current liabilities. Tangible-net-

[23] See, for instance, Emery and Ou (2004), May, Rosenthal, and Verde (2007), Solomon (2007), and Zhang (2009).

worth covenants specify a minimum level of net tangible assets. Capital expenditure covenants require the borrower to limit capital expenditures to a certain amount.

Covenants can be either incurrence or maintenance covenants. Incurrence covenants prohibit the borrower to actively breach a covenant. Maintenance covenants are significantly stricter: They require that the borrower takes the initiative to avoid that a covenant is breached. For instance, if a leverage covenant demands a certain maximum debt-to-cash-flow ratio and this ratio is exceeded because the borrower's cash flow worsens, this would constitute a breach of a maintenance covenant but not of an incurrence covenant. A breach of the latter would only occur if the maximum ratio is exceeded due to a particular action of the borrower, for instance the issuance of additional debt.

Leveraged loans are generally subject to maintenance covenants whereas bonds come along with incurrence covenants. Together, collateral- and covenant-related provisions in leveraged loans thus limit lenders' risk exposure much more efficaciously than those in bonds. This makes leveraged loans the cheapest source of funding for sub-investment grade firms and is one of the reasons why they enjoy such a great popularity.

4.2.4 Coupons and Prepayment

Leveraged loans pay floating rate coupons. These are composed of LIBOR (or another interbank rate, depending on the loan's currency) plus a certain spread (i.e. risk premium) and are typically payable quarterly. Floating rate coupons provide a hedge against interest rate risk: If interest rates rise, so does the coupon and vice versa. Further, the spread of leveraged loans often is not constant but moves according to a predefined pricing grid: If the borrower's credit condition improves, for instance indicated by a decline of financial leverage and/or a rating upgrade, the spread decreases and vice versa.

Leveraged loans commonly mature between seven and ten years after issuance. Their effective life, however, tends to be much shorter as borrowers are typically allowed to prepay or "call" the loan at any time at no or a limited premium. Prepayment is generally seen as a negative by lenders. This is because borrowers tend to prepay when a refinancing will reduce their interest expenses but otherwise avoid such an action. Floating-rate coupons eliminate the incentive to prepay in response to a decline in interest rates. However, prepayment often is advantageous to the borrower if his credit quality has improved, as pricing grids typically foresee only a limited reduction in coupons. For lenders, this means that they bear most of the downside but retain limited upside.

Bonds mostly pay fixed rate coupons, with zero coupons or floating rate coupons being less common. Their maturity lies mostly between seven and ten years, too, with no right to prepay during the first half of their life and only at a premium price thereafter. Usually, this is par plus 50% of the coupon in the first year prepayment is allowed, declining linearly to par until maturity. Less frequently, bonds are convertible into the borrower's equity or contain a put provision that allows lenders to demand early prepayment.

4.3 Standard Terms of Single-Name Credit Default Swaps

It is the objective of this section to work out the major differences between LCDSs and CDSs based on the foregone comparison of respective underlyings. To this end, Section 4.3.1 first gives an overview of the framework documentation that governs all non-bespoke (L)CDS transactions. Section 4.3.2 then discusses investors' preferences as to the properties of LCDSs. These had significant influence on how standard language was drafted and are thus responsible for several conceptual differences between i) U.S. vs. European LCDSs and ii) LCDSs vs. CDSs. Sections 4.3.3 to 4.3.5 analyze these differences in as far as they are relevant for the purpose of this thesis, leaving aside many technicalities. For a more detailed treatment of the topic, the interested reader is referred to Schläfer and Uhrig-Homburg (2010a).

4.3.1 Framework Documentation

Participants in the OTC derivatives market generally conclude their transactions under the "Master Agreement" published by ISDA. It serves as an umbrella bilateral contract and is currently available in the form of the 1992 and the 2002 edition.[24] Its terms and conditions comprise, among other things, provisions related to payment netting, general representations, and covenants.[25] The Master Agreement includes a "Schedule"[26] in which parties may modify these terms and conditions and chose to apply or discard certain elections. In addition to the Master Agreement, ISDA has published separate sets of definitions for particular types of derivatives. Each of these sets incorporates a "Confirmation" which parties use to document the agreed details of a particular transaction. As a result of this architecture, the Master Agreement, together with each possible set of definitions and the associated Confirmation, is capable of covering a wide range of derivative instruments.

The 2003 Credit Derivatives Definitions[27] are the relevant set of definitions for documenting CDS transactions. In the following, the 2002 Master Agreement in conjunction with the 2003

[24] See ISDA (1992 and 2002a).
[25] For detail on the Master Agreement see, for instance, Harding (2003) and ISDA (2002c).
[26] See ISDA (2002b).
[27] See ISDA (2003).

Credit Derivatives Definitions are therefore referred to as "CDS Standard Terms". CDS Standard Terms apply to both, the U.S. and the European CDS market.

CDS Standard Terms are equally applicable to LCDS transactions. However, given the special nature of leveraged loans as reference obligations under LCDSs, amendments to the 2003 Credit Derivatives Definitions became inevitable. In the U.S., such amendments were first published by ISDA in June 2006 in form of the "Syndicated Secured Loan Credit Default Swap Standard Terms Supplement and Confirmation"[28], and a revised version became available in May 2007[29]. In the following, the 2002 Master Agreement in conjunction with the 2003 Credit Derivatives Definitions and the 2007 U.S. set of LCDS definitions are referred to as "U.S. LCDS Standard Terms".

	U.S. LCDS Standard Terms	European LCDS Standard Terms	CDS Standard Terms
Product-Specific Documentation	Syndicated Secured Loan Credit Default Swap Standard Terms Supplement and Confirmation as of May 2007	Standard Terms Supplement for Use with Credit Derivative Transactions on Leveraged Loans and Confirmation as of March 2008	N/A
General Framework Documentation for Credit Derivatives Transactions	2003 Credit Derivatives Definitions and Confirmation		
General Framework Documentation for OTC Derivatives Transactions	2002 ISDA Master Agreement and Schedule		

Table 4.2: Framework Documentation for LCDS and CDS Transactions
This table shows an overview of the framework documentation under which non-bespoke LCDS and CDS transactions are concluded. Together, the relevant documents are referred to as "U.S. LCDS Standard Terms", "European LCDS Standard Terms", and "CDS Standard Terms", respectively.

In Europe, ISDA published the "Standard Terms Supplement for Use With Credit Derivative Transactions on Leveraged Loans and Confirmation" in July 2007[30], and a revised version, which catered more to the requirements of non-banks, became available in March 2008[31]. In the following, the 2002 Master Agreement in conjunction with the 2003 Credit Derivatives

[28] See ISDA (2006a and 2006b).
[29] See ISDA (2007a and 2007b).
[30] See ISDA (2007c and 2007d).
[31] See ISDA (2008a and 2008b).

Definitions and the 2008 European set of LCDS definitions are referred to as "European LCDS Standard Terms". Table 4.2 provides an overview of mentioned documents.

4.3.2 Investors' Requirements

It was mentioned in Section 4.1 that investors may have divergent motivations for participating in the LCDS market. For this reason, different preferences exist with regard to the structure of LCDSs.[32] In particular, two quite distinct investor groups can be identified: The first seeks a tool for *trading* the credit risk associated with syndicated secured loans, the second is primarily interested in *hedging* this risk. Members of the first group, often hedge funds, managers of synthetic Collateralized Loan Obligations (CLOs), insurance companies, and other institutional investors, are concerned with liquidity and ease of transfer. They want LCDSs to reflect the *general* credit risk associated with a particular reference entity. This in turn means that the LCDS should continue even if the reference entity repays the loan that serves as reference obligation. Members of the second group, such as financial institutions, often seek an efficient hedging tool that fulfils the requirements of Basel II. They want to use LCDSs to hedge away the credit risk associated with a *specific* loan, which they, as syndicate members, have on their books. If the reference entity repays this loan, there is no longer a risk to be hedged and the LCDS should terminate, as well. Also, they require the inclusion of "restructuring" as a credit event, or otherwise the hedge would not provide full capital relieve according to the rules of Basel II.

The discussion in the next three sections shows that these requirements have left their mark on how provisions in LCDS Standard Terms have been drafted, most importantly those referring to the reference entity, reference obligation, contract cancellation, and credit events. Generally speaking, U.S. LCDS Standard Terms are more trader-friendly, due to the traditionally strong position of the institutional investor base in the U.S. whereas European LCDS Standard Terms are more hedger-friendly, or at least provide some flexibility that recognizes the particular requirements of banks which still play a dominant role in the European syndicated loan market.

4.3.3 Reference Entity and Reference Obligation

Under U.S. LCDS Standard Terms, parties specify a particular reference entity in the Confirmation. They then have the choice between either i) stipulating as reference obligation a par-

[32] A discussion of the legal aspects of LCDS and the motivation of market participants can also be found in Artmann and Bartlam (2007a and 2007b).

ticular loan or tranche of a loan issued by that reference entity or ii) electing "secured list" and specifying a "designated priority" which is either "first lien", "second lien" or "third lien".[33] In the case of ii), which is the market standard, the reference obligation is the loan which is specified as the currently applicable reference obligation in the "relevant secured list"[34] administrated by Markit.[35]

The procedure for filling and keeping up-to-date the relevant secured list is described in the "Syndicated Secured Loan Polling Rules"[36] as published by Markit in December 2007. In short, this procedure is as follows: Any of the participants eligible for loan polling, called "specified dealers"[37] may request Markit, currently the "secured list publisher"[38], to initiate a poll with respect to a particular loan. If a poll has been initiated, Markit asks specified dealers whether the loan in question i) is currently outstanding (also applicable to unfunded lending commitments), ii) arises under a syndicated loan agreement, and iii) has a priority of at least third lien. Further, specified dealers are asked to classify the loan's priority (first to third lien). If a quorum of specified dealers affirms questions i) to iii), that quorum's classification of the loan's priority is recorded. For a particular reference entity, Markit then composes the relevant secured list, which details the syndicated secured loans issued by that reference entity together with their priority as ascertained by previous polls. Finally, for each reference entity and for each of the three priorities, Markit, in consultation with specified dealers, selects from this list a suitable loan (if one or more loans of a given priority exist) that then serves as reference obligation. This process is repeated whenever required, so that the relevant secured lists are up to date with the currently outstanding loans of reference entities. The reference obligation thusly specified is then applicable under a U.S. LCDS if "secured list" and a designated priority are stipulated, extricating parties from the task of identifying a particular obligation that is representative of the issuer's credit risk.

A similar procedure, called "syndicated secured dispute resolution", comes into effect if any of the parties disputes that the reference obligation satisfies the "syndicated secured" characteristic.[39] A loan is syndicated secured if it is an "obligation […] i) that arises under a syndicated loan agreement and ii) that […] trades as a loan of the designated priority […] in the

33 See ISDA (2007b), p2.
34 Published on http://www.markit.com.
35 See ISDA (2007a), Sec1.
36 See Markit (2007).
37 Many of the major international banks active in credit derivatives trading are specified dealers. Rules for polling eligibility are detailed in Markit (2007), pA-1.
38 The secured list publisher is appointed by specified dealers. See ISDA (2007a), Sec1.
39 See ISDA (2007a), Sec1.

primary or secondary loan market".[40] This means that unfunded revolvers or letter of credit commitments can be valid reference obligations.

Based on the Syndicated Secured Loan Polling Rules and the syndicated secured dispute resolution, specified dealers and not parties decide whether a loan is syndicated secured and what its designated priority is and determine the then current reference obligation for a particular reference entity. This process introduces consistency and certainty with regard to the legal interpretation of "syndicated" and "secured" and creates a standardized product where the reference obligation of a particular reference entity and designated priority is consistent across the market.[41]

Under European LCDS Standard Terms, the determination of the reference obligation is by way of identifying in the Confirmation a specific loan agreement of the reference entity, the "reference credit agreement". Further, parties have the option to specify a particular "tranche or facility which constitutes a loan" under the reference credit agreement which also "may comprise of a credit facility with an undrawn commitment". If only a reference credit agreement is specified, "each tranche or facility which constitutes a loan under the reference credit agreement" is a reference obligation. The reference entity itself is not directly specified but is automatically defined as "any person [...] who is a borrower" under the reference obligation.[42] It should be noted that European LCDS Standard Term (in contrast to U.S. LCDS Standard Terms) do not expressly require the reference obligation to be syndicated or secured. They are, however, intended to be used for leveraged loans which are, as discussed earlier, virtually always syndicated and secured.

The basic structure of U.S. and European LCDS Standard Terms is thus quite different: U.S. LCDS Standard Terms emphasize the general credit risk associated with the reference entity and are thus *reference entity-based*. European LCDS Standard Terms, on the other hand, focus on the credit risk associated with a particular reference obligation and are rather *reference obligation-based*. The different requirements of market participants, being trading or hedging, have thus found their expression in the way LCDS Standard Terms have been drafted.

CDSs can be set up either as reference entity- or reference obligation-based contracts: Under CDS Standard Terms, parties specify a particular reference entity in the Confirmation.[43] Also, they may specify a reference obligation with a particular priority but are not required to do so.

---

[40] See ISDA (2007a), Sec4.
[41] See LSTA (2007).
[42] See ISDA (2008a), Sec1.
[43] See ISDA (2003), Sec2.1.

If they do not, reference obligations effectively are all unsubordinated obligations of the reference entity.[44]

4.3.4 Contract Cancellation

As noted earlier, leveraged loans can generally be prepaid at no or at a limited premium. This prompts the question as to what happens to an LCDS if its reference obligation ceases to exist. U.S. LCDS Standard Terms are designed to avoid, if possible, that the LCDS cancels in this event. To that end, they dispose of "an elaborate substitution mechanism which seeks to ensure that the LCDS is only called as a last resort"[45]. This mechanism comes into effect if parties have either i) specified a particular reference obligation which has been repaid or terminated or, which, in the opinion of the "calculation agent"[46], has been materially reduced or fails to satisfy the syndicated secured characteristic discussed earlier or ii) stipulated "secured list" and the relevant secured list is withdrawn.[47] Such a withdrawal will, however, only occur if none of its constituents remain. If, on the other hand, the relevant secured list just changes but still lists one or more loans of the reference entity, this will not trigger the substitution mechanism.

In either case, the calculation agent will commence the search for a "substitute reference obligation" which has to satisfy the syndicated secured characteristic. If such a loan is found, it replaces the prior reference obligation and the LCDS continues to live. Only if such a loan cannot be found will the LCDS cancel.

European LCDS Standard Terms are designed to avoid cancellation, as well. However, parties have the flexibility to tie the LCDS more closely to the fate of a particular loan: In the Confirmation, "continuity" applies by default but parties can stipulate that it shall not. If continuity applies and the reference obligation is repaid in full, the calculation agent will determine whether a refinancing has occurred and if so, whether there is a "successor credit agreement" to the reference credit agreement. Each tranche or facility under the successor credit agreement which is secured is a substitute reference obligation. This substitution mechanism avoids legal uncertainty and the LCDS will only terminate if no successor credit agreement (and therefore no substitute reference obligation) exists or if no refinancing has occurred. If conti-

[44] See ISDA (2003), Sec2.3 and Sec 2.19.
[45] See Artmann and Bartlam (2007a), p290.
[46] In the Confirmation, parties specify a calculation agent who takes on certain administrative duties with regard to an (L)CDS transaction. Often, the calculation agent is the protection seller.
[47] See ISDA (2007a), Sec1.

nuity does not apply and the reference obligation is repaid in full, the LCDS terminates at zero costs for parties.[48]

Determining whether or not a successor credit agreement exists requires information which is, at least in the European leveraged loan market, private information, only available to syndicate members.[49] For this reason, European LCDS Standard Terms include provisions that allow either party to declare that there is a successor credit agreement in case the calculation agent does not dispose of the relevant private information.[50] If neither the calculation agent nor parties dispose of the information to make such a declaration, the European LCDS terminates at zero costs for parties.

The 2007 edition of European LCDS Standard Terms did not foresee a substitution at all but stipulated cancellation in any event, should the reference obligation cease to exist.[51] This reflected the particular needs of market participants such as banks, who intended to use LCDSs primarily as a hedging product. In contrast, European LCDS Standard Terms as they stand now should also appeal to investors concerned with taking a view on the credit risk associated with a particular borrower, rather than with a particular loan of that borrower. Such a specification should generally result in higher liquidity and ease of transfer and is comparable to U.S. LCDS Standard Terms which, as mentioned earlier, have a strong focus on trader-friendliness.

If, under CDS Standard Terms, a reference obligation is specified and is redeemed in whole or has been materially reduced, the calculation agent commences the search for a substitute reference obligation. The CDS does not terminate early in any event and even if no substitute reference obligation is found, the protection buyer continues to pay the premium until the CDS terminates. CDS Standard Terms are thus quite different from LCDS Standard Terms in that CDS contracts *never* cancel.[52]

4.3.5 Credit Events

To determine whether a credit event has occurred, it is necessary to define what circumstances cause such an event but also which of the reference entity's obligations must be affected. To this end, the 2003 Credit Derivatives Definitions specify six possible credit events and six "obligation categories".[53] Whether a credit event has occurred will be tested, with the excep-

---

48 See ISDA (2008a), Sec6.e.
49 See Artmann and Bartlam (2007b).
50 See ISDA (2008a), Sec6.e.a.
51 See Artmann and Bartlam (2007b).
52 See Galiani, Gallo, Jónsson, and Kakodkar (2006).
53 See ISDA (2003), Sec2.19 and Sec4.2-4.7.

tion of “bankruptcy” with respect to those obligations that are part of the relevant obligation category.

Credit events are:

- “Bankruptcy”: The reference entity has become insolvent or is unable to pay its debts or is dissolved or liquidated other than under a merger or consolidation.
- “Obligation acceleration”: An obligation has become due and payable immediately due to occurrence of a default or a similar condition.
- “Obligation default”: An obligation has become capable of being declared due and payable due to the occurrence of a default or a similar condition.
- “Failure to pay”: After the expiration of any applicable grace period, the reference entity fails to make payments when due and payable under an obligation.
- “Repudiation/moratorium”: An authorized person of the reference entity or a governmental authority repudiates or rejects the validity of an obligation or declares a moratorium, standstill, roll-over, or deferral with regard to such an obligation.
- “Restructuring”: With regard to an obligation one or more of the following occurs: “i) A reduction in the rate or amount of interest payable [...]; ii) a reduction in the amount of principal or premium payable at maturity or at scheduled redemption dates; iii) a postponement or other deferral of a date or dates for either a) the payment of accrual of interest or b) the payment of principal or premium;” iv) an adverse change in the ranking or priority of the obligation; or v) certain changes in the currency of any payment of interest or principal. However, these criteria only apply if they result “from deterioration in the creditworthiness or financial condition of the reference entity”. Also, to avoid that a restructuring credit event is triggered by a bilateral renegotiation of obligation terms between the borrower and a single lender, the obligation further has to be “held by more than three holders that are not affiliates of each other”.[54]

Obligation categories are:

- “Payment”: “Any obligation, whether present or future, contingent or otherwise, for the payment or repayment of money.” Payment is the broadest of all obligation categories.
- “Borrowed money”: “Any obligation, excluding an obligation under a revolving credit arrangement for which there are no outstanding, unpaid drawings for the payment or repayment of money”.

[54] See ISDA (2003), Sec4.9.a.

- "Reference obligations only": "Any obligation that is a reference obligation".
- "Bond": Any bond that is included in borrowed money.
- "Loan": Any loan that is included in borrowed money. According to the definition of borrowed money, this does not include undrawn revolvers or letter of credit commitments.
- "Bond or Loan": Either bond or loan as defined above.

Under U.S. LCDS Standard Terms, credit events are always bankruptcy and failure to pay and the obligation category is always borrowed money.[55] This means that a credit event can be triggered by any obligation of the reference entity (with the notable exception of undrawn revolvers).

Under European LCDS Standard Terms, credit events are always bankruptcy, failure to pay and restructuring. The obligation category is always "reference obligations only" without any obligation characteristics.[56] Thus, if failure to pay or restructuring occurs in a loan other than the reference obligation, this would not trigger a credit event. Further, the definition of "restructuring" has been amended to reflect the secured nature of leverage loans: In addition to the criteria mentioned above, restructuring is triggered in the event of release or discharge of all security of the reference obligation, unless i) such security is immediately replaced or ii) the proceeds of the release or discharge are used to repay secured debt with a priority or ranking equal or senior to the reference obligation.[57]

Under CDS Standard Terms, parties elect in the Confirmation the credit events that shall apply.[58] For U.S. and European CDS transactions, it has however become market convention not to include obligation acceleration and obligation default. Typically, repudiation / moratorium is used only if the reference entity is a sovereign. Thus, frequently used credit events are bankruptcy, failure to pay, and restructuring. Further, parties may elect any one of the six obligation categories but it is market convention to choose borrowed money.[59]

Restructuring differs from all other credit events in that it is not associated with a default of the reference entity. This has two important implications: First, the reference entity's obligations continue to live, albeit they will likely trade at a discount to compensate lenders for the financial distress that has led to the restructuring event. Such a discount will generally be more pronounced for obligations with longer maturities. Second, the reference entity's ap-

[55] See ISDA (2007a), Sec3.
[56] See ISDA (2008a), Sec3.
[57] See ISDA (2008a), Sec6.h.iii.
[58] See ISDA (2003), Sec2.19.
[59] See Galiani, Gallo, Jónsson, and Kakodkar (2006).

proval continues to be necessary for a transfer of consent-required loans. Protection sellers will dislike delivery of such loans as their resale opportunities can be restricted.

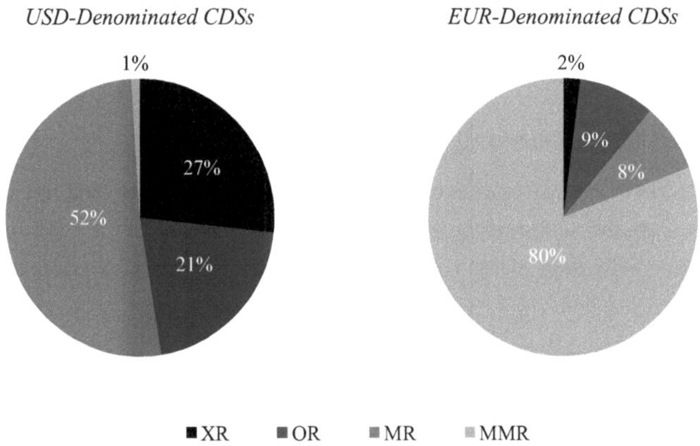

Figure 4.2: Restructuring Definitions in Non-Sovereign CDSs
This figure illustrates the frequency of restructuring definitions (no restructuring (XR), old restructuring (OR), modified restructuring (MR), and modified modified restructuring (MMR)) in 3,112 USD- and EUR-denominated CDSs on senior unsecured bonds and loans of financial institutions and corporate issuers as quoted by Markit.

If restructuring applies, parties therefore have to specify the maximum maturity and the transferability characteristics of the deliverable obligation. These specifications have become known as "old restructuring" (OR), "modified restructuring" (MR), and "modified modified restructuring" (MMR). Under OR there are no requirements regarding transferability and the maturity of the deliverable obligation. However, parties typically limit the latter to 30 years to avoid delivery of perpetual bonds, as these could potentially be treated unfavorably in a restructuring event.[60] Under MR, deliverable obligations must be "fully transferable" which means transferable "without the consent of any person being required" and their maturity must not exceed 30 months.[61] Under MMR, deliverable obligations need only be "conditionally transferable", meaning that "consent [to a transfer] may not be unreasonably withheld or delayed" and their maturity must not exceed 60 months if the deliverable obligation is a restructured obligation and 30 months otherwise.[62]

60 See Galiani, Gallo, Jónsson, and Kakodkar (2006).
61 See ISDA (2003), Sec2.32.
62 See ISDA (2003), Sec2.33.

Figure 4.2 illustrates the frequency of restructuring definitions in non-sovereign CDSs for the U.S. and European market. The numbers show that virtually all EUR-denominated CDSs include restructuring as a credit event and that MMR, being more protection buyer-friendly a definition than MR, is used most frequently (80%). For USD-denominated CDSs, on the other hand, "no restructuring" (XR) and MR dominate (52 and 27%) with the share of MMR being negligible.

	U.S. LCDS Standard Terms	European LCDS Standard Terms	CDS Standard Terms
Credit Events			
Bankruptcy	Mandatory	Mandatory	Eligible and Common
Obligation Acceleration			Eligible but less Common
Obligation Default			Eligible but less Common
Failure to Pay	Mandatory	Mandatory	Eligible and Common
Repudiation/Moratorium			Eligible but less Common
Restructuring			
XR	Mandatory		Eligible but less Common
OR		Mandatory	Eligible but less Common
MR			Eligible and Common (U.S.)
MMR			Eligible and Common (Europe)
Obligation Categories			
Payment			Eligible but less Common
Borrowed Money	Mandatory		Eligible and Common
Reference Obligations Only		Mandatory	Eligible but less Common
Bond			Eligible but less Common
Loan			Eligible but less Common
Bond or Loan			Eligible but less Common

■ Mandatory ■ Eligible and Common ■ Eligible but less Common

Table 4.3: Credit Event Definitions under LCDS and CDS Standard Terms
This table shows an overview of credit events and obligation categories that are mandatory, eligible and common, or eligible but less common under U.S. and European LCDS Standard Terms, as well as under CDS Standard Terms.

Table 4.3 summarizes above discussion: LCDS Standard Terms do not provide flexibility with regard to the specification of obligation categories and credit events. European LCDS Standard Terms are reference obligation-based in that credit events are only triggered if they occur in the reference obligation, but not in any other obligation of the reference entity. Further, by including restructuring, they cater to the needs of banks who desire a hedging product that provides full capital relief under Basel II. U.S. LCDS Standard Terms, on the other hand, are reference entity-based: A failure to pay credit event is triggered if it occurs in any borrowed money obligation (i.e. almost any obligation) of the reference entity. CDS Standard Terms provide parties with a maximum of flexibility. In practice, however, specifications are identical to U.S. LCDSs, the only exception being restructuring, which is frequently included, both, in the U.S. and in Europe.

4.4 Key Topics Revisited

The previous two sections have shown that LCDS and CDS Standard Terms differ importantly in several key aspects, owed to the diverging nature of underlyings. In particular, discrepancies arise from provisions referring to contract cancellation, restructuring as a credit event, and the definition of "obligation category", as summarized in Table 4.4. If these discrepancies have a significant impact, ratios of LCDS and CDS premia are not solely a function of implied recovery rates, and estimation results will be distorted accordingly. In the following, it is therefore examined for each of the three mentioned topics what the effect on premia should be and whether pro-forma adjustments exist that make aberrant provisions comparable.

	LCDS Standard Terms		
	U.S.	Europe	CDS Standard Terms
Contract Cancellation	If no substitute reference obligation is found	If continuity does not apply or if no substitute reference obligation is found. 2007 edition of European Standard Terms: Always	Never
Restructuring as a Credit Event	XR	OR	XR, OR, MR, MMR
Obligation Category	Borrowed money	Reference obligation only	Borrowed money

Table 4.4: Key Differences Between LCDS and CDS Standard Terms

This table shows an overview of the differences between LCDS and CDS Standard Terms that are relevant for the purpose of this thesis. These arise from provisions regarding contract cancellation, restructuring as a credit event, and the definition of "obligation category".

Contract Cancellation

It was argued in Section 4.2.4 that prepayment rates and changes in a borrower's credit quality are negatively related and that this affects lenders' profit and loss profile negatively. A similar line of argument is applicable to LCDS cancellation and the situation of protection sellers: If a prepayment event results in the LCDS being canceled precisely at the time the reference obligation's credit quality improves, the protection seller will no longer receive the (now comparatively generous) premium payments. In the opposite case, however, he will have to continue providing protection, and this protection has become more valuable. Ceteris paribus, the protection seller will therefore require a mark-up on the LCDS premium as a compensation for cancellation risk. If, however, prepayment is caused by events such as a merger, an acquisition (M&A), or a leveraged buyout (LBO), the protection seller should not be disadvantaged systematically, assuming that the probability of such events is not systematically related to the borrower's credit quality.

Mark-ups to compensate for cancellation should be higher for worse ratings of the reference entity and not just in absolute, but also in relative terms. This is because i) for lower-rated firms, an improvement in credit quality is more likely than for higher-rated firms, and therefore a refinancing is also more likely and ii) in absolute terms, cancellation hurts protection sellers more if LCDS premia are high. Elizalde (2007) shows in a rather simplistic model setup that this is indeed so: He assumes that in the event of a refinancing, the LCDS cancels with certainty and that default and refinancing probabilities are positively related. For each rating category, he then derives the term structure of probabilities of default from historical cumulative default rates as published by S&P. His results suggest that if the reference entity's S&P rating is between A and B+, a reasonable mark-up to compensate for cancellation is less than 2% of the LCDS premium. For ratings B and below, however, such a mark-up increases exponentially, rising beyond 10% for CCC-rated borrowers.

If the issuer moves to investment grade and thus, by definition, no longer uses leveraged loans as a funding source, no successor credit agreement will exist and the LCDS will cancel surely. This, however, suggests that the issuer was rated close to investment grade prior to the upgrade, in which case, as just argued, costs to the protection seller are rather negligible.

If, however, the borrower retains his sub-investment grade status, he is very likely to refinance. Thus, a successor credit agreement becomes available precisely in those situations in which it is needed most urgently. It is then crucial whether applicable LCDS Standard Terms stipulate that a substitute reference obligation comes into effect, or not. It was mentioned in Section 4.3.4 that such is the case in any event under U.S. LCDS Standard Terms whereas under the 2008 edition of European Standard Terms only if "continuity" applies. The LCDS then continues to live and the protection seller is not disadvantaged systematically.

Under the 2007 edition of European Standard Terms, or under the 2008 edition if "continuity" does not apply, however, the protection seller forfeits the upside and will thus demand a compensation. In conclusion, prepayment should result in a negligible or no mark-up on premia of U.S. LCDSs whereas such a mark-up could be quite substantial for premia of some European LCDSs. Figure 4.3 illustrates this line of argument graphically.

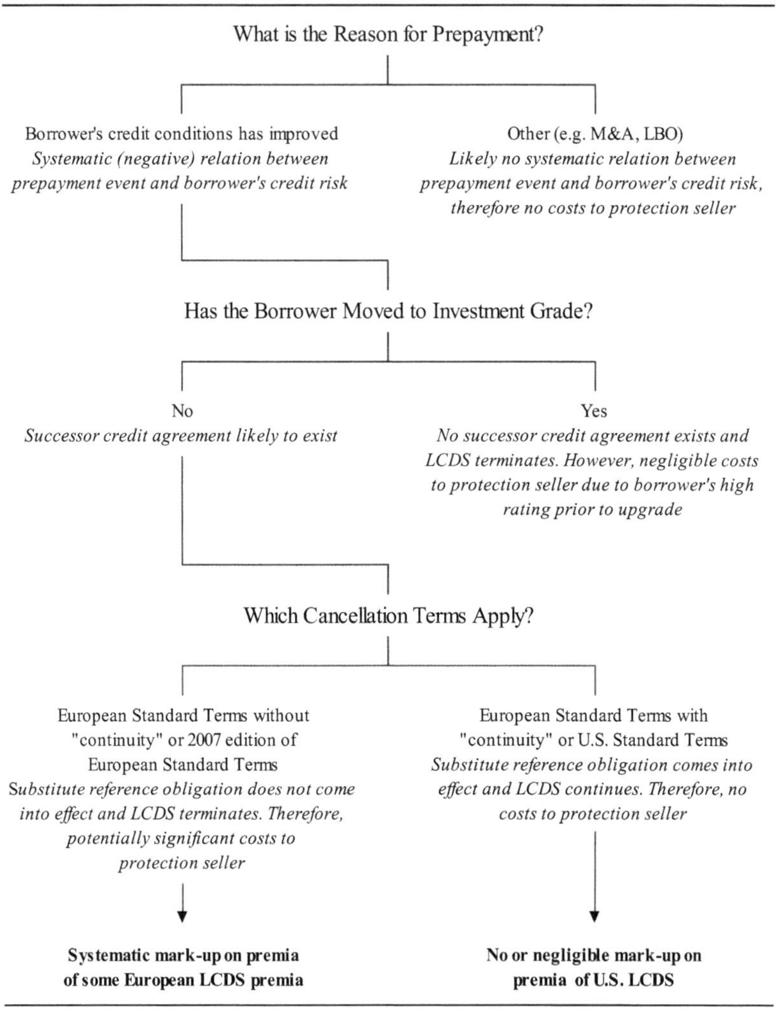

Figure 4.3: The Impact of Prepayment on LCDS Premia

This figure illustrates that prepayment can produce a significant mark-up only on premia of some European LCDSs. Premia of U.S. LCDSs, on the other hand, should not be affected materially by prepayment because U.S. LCDS Standard Terms avoid cancellation in those circumstances that would otherwise be associated with significant costs to protection sellers.

Restructuring as a Credit Event and Obligation Category

Credit events and obligation categories determine, to some extent, the probability with which payments under the protection leg of an (L)CDS come into effect. It is easy to see that, ceteris paribus, including a greater number of credit events or stipulating a broader definition of "obligation category" increases this probability and vice versa. Thus, two (L)CDSs referencing the same borrower could trade at different implied probabilities of default, if terms deviate.

If restructuring applies, it further matters which maturities and transferability characteristics are permissible with respect to the deliverable obligation. While this does not affect the probability of default itself, protection sellers will disapprove of these terms being too lenient, and accordingly the mark-up on premia should be higher for OR than for MR or MMR.

(L)CDS quotes provided by data vendors such as Markit or ValuSpread typically are averages of mid-market quotes submitted by a number of contributors. For instance, Markit currently sources quotes from more than 60 financial institutions world-wide, although the number of contributors for any given (L)CDS usually is much smaller.[63] To make CDS quotes that are based on distinct restructuring definitions comparable, Markit applies certain adjustment factors that are based on the global average percentage difference between these definitions. As Figure 4.4 illustrates, the factor to adjust from XR to OR is 1.1299, and, as one would expect, factors to adjust to MMR and MR are somewhat smaller (1.0847 and 1.0565, respectively). Berndt, Jarrow, and Kang (2007) examine CDS data provided by ValuSpread and arrive at similar figures. For instance, they find that MR trades at a mark-up of 5.69% relative to XR, which is virtually identical to the adjustment made by Markit.

This suggests that different restructuring definitions can be accounted for in a straightforward manner, for instance by marking CDS premia, where necessary, down to XR (if paired with U.S. LCDS premia) or up to OR (if paired with European LCDS premia). A similar procedure to adjust divergent obligation categories is, however, not at hand, and it is quite unclear how material such an adjustment would be.

To conclude, pairs of U.S. LCDSs and CDSs should represent a fairly uncontaminated measure of implied recovery: Prepayment plays a relatively minor role in U.S. LCDSs since a substitute reference obligation comes into effect where crucial, and CDS premia can be proforma adjusted to XR based on a well-established procedure. As for pairs of European LCDSs and CDSs, the picture is, however, a different one. Even though European LCDS Standard Terms allow parties to stipulate "continuity", such a choice is not mandatory. Furthermore, historical data may comprise instruments that were concluded under the predecessor terms

[63] See Markit (2006).

which foresaw cancellation in any event. Also, the effect of "reference obligation only" as obligation category is hard to quantify and a sensible pro-forma adjustment is not available. For these reasons, the use of European LCDSs will not be pursued further.

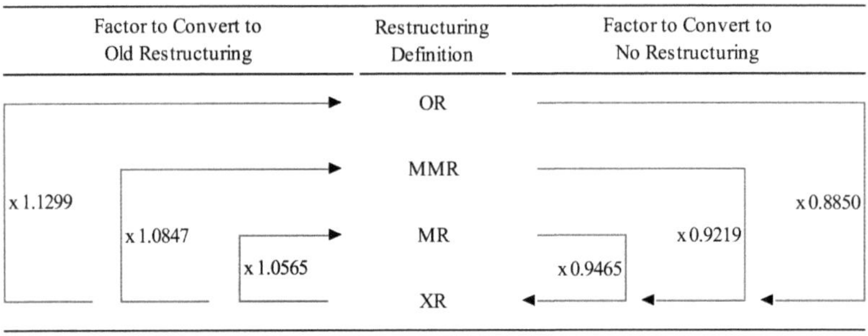

Figure 4.4: Conversion Factors for Restructuring Definitions
This figure illustrates adjustment factors, as applied by Markit, to make different restructuring definitions comparable. Ceteris paribus, no restructuring (XR), being the most protection-seller friendly definition, results in the lowest CDS premium whereas old restructuring (OR), being the most protection-buyer friendly definition, results in the highest CDS premium. Modified restructuring (MR) and modified modified restructuring (MMR) lie in between. See Markit (2006).

5 Implementation and Results

The discussion in Chapter 4 revealed that an uncontaminated measure of implied recovery, as put forth by Eq. (3.8), can be derived either i) from two CDSs referencing bonds of different priorities or ii) from a U.S. LCDS and a CDS, provided that divergent restructuring definitions are accounted for. In Section 5.1, the universe of available (L)CDS data is screened, and firms are identified on which either pair is outstanding at a given point in time. This allows it to construct suitable sets of historical premia for the implementation of the approach. Further, issuers' capital structure is analyzed such that the priority of claims can be accounted for.

Section 5.2 then customizes the setup of the model to the data at hand and outlines the empirical specification as well as the calibration procedure. Section 5.3 presents estimates of implied recovery, both firm-wide and instrument specific, and examines the effect of debt cushion, changes in the economic environment, and ratings. Section 5.4 assesses robustness by implementing two alternative model specifications, an alternative calibration procedure, and by setting implied figures in relation to historical realizations.

Finally, Section 5.5 illustrates how estimates of implied expected recovery rates can be used to derive implied probabilities of default. Results are then used to study the relation of both factors under the pricing measure as well as to determine investors' degree of aversion to default risk.

5.1 Data and Descriptive Statistics

5.1.1 Construction of Samples

Mid-market premia for a total of 4,109 USD-, EUR-, GBP-, and JPY-denominated CDSs with a maturity of five years are obtained from Markit. To assure that capital structure analyses are comparable across firms, issuers are required to report according to U.S.-GAAP, effectively reducing the relevant universe to 2,431 USD-denominated CDSs.[64] Figure 5.1 illustrates the priority of reference obligations in this subset: The overwhelming majority of CDSs references senior unsecured debt with senior subordinated and senior secured bonds being refe-

[64] This does not obviate large non-U.S. firms that, in addition to reporting according to domestic accounting principles, also report according to U.S.-GAAP, because these firms are likely to have USD-denominated CDSs outstanding.

renced relatively seldom and the share of other priorities being negligible. Further analysis shows that for 62 firms, senior unsecured and senior subordinated CDSs are outstanding at the same time. 35 of these firms, however, are financial institutions and must be discarded to assure comparability of capital structure analyses. Another ten firms are eliminated because concurrent quotes for both instruments are available for less than 20 weeks. This leaves a total of 17 firms, henceforth referred to as "Sample 1". Restructuring definitions are either XR or MR without exception. Following Markit (2006), MR is pro-forma adjusted to XR by multiplying premia with 0.9465.

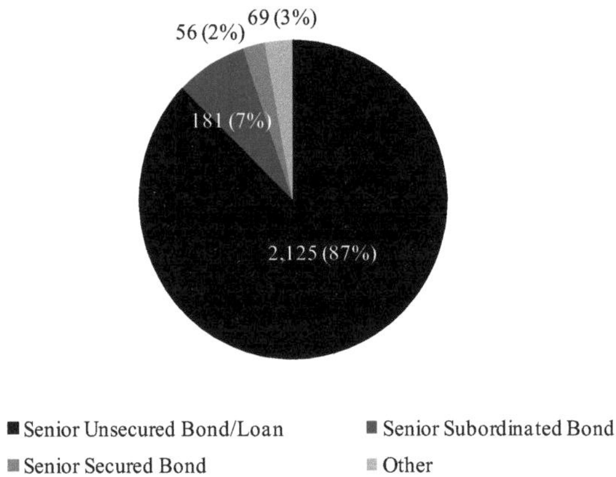

Figure 5.1: The Priority of Reference Obligations in Non-Sovereign CDSs
This figure illustrates the priority of reference obligations in 2,431 USD-denominated CDSs on obligations of financial institutions and corporate issuers as quoted by Markit.

For another 15 firms, senior secured and senior unsecured CDSs are outstanding at the same time. Unfortunately, concurrent quotes for at least 20 weeks are observed only for five of them, and the sample is therefore discarded. Other combinations are observed very rarely and are not pursued further.

Mid-market premia for 37 liquidly-traded U.S. LCDSs with a maturity of five years are obtained from a major investment bank. For 25 of these firms, senior unsecured CDSs are outstanding at the same time, other combinations are not observed. Eliminating five firms for which concurrent quotes are available for less than 20 weeks leaves a total of 20 firms, henceforth referred to as "Sample 2". Restructuring definitions for the senior unsecured CDSs are either XR or MR in all cases, and, where applicable, premia are pro-forma adjusted as described above.

Table 5.1 shows an overview of resulting samples: Sample 1 (senior unsecured CDSs and senior subordinated CDSs) comprises 17 U.S. firms, two of which have an investment grade rating. Data lie between January 2001 and December 2007, and on average 163 pairs of end-of-week premia are observed for each firm. Sample 2 (LCDSs and senior unsecured CDSs) comprises 20 U.S. firms, each with a sub-investment grade rating.[65] Data lie between May 2006 and July 2008, and on average 65 pairs of end-of-week premia are observed for each firm. Due to the relative newness of the LCDS market, earlier information is not available or of limited quality. Constituents of both samples belong to a variety of industries including consumer goods & services, technology, industrials, media, automotive, and healthcare. For a breakdown of key statistics by firm, the reader is referred to Appendix B.

	Sample 1	Sample 2
Instruments	Senior unsecured CDSs, senior subordinated CDSs	LCDSs, senior unsecured CDSs
Constituents	17 U.S. non-financial issuers	20 U.S. non-financial issuers
Rating (IG/sub-IG)	2/12	0/20
First - Last Observation	Jan-2001 - Dec-2007	May-2006 - Jul-2008
Avg. Count of Pairs (Weekly)	163	65

Table 5.1: Overview of Samples

This table shows an overview of the two samples on which all analyses in this thesis are based. Ratings are Moody's corporate family ratings. Three of the firms in Sample 1 carry no such rating.

5.1.2 Credit Default Swap Premia

Table 5.2 gives an overview of premia by sample, averaged over all firms and the entire observation period. As one would expect, seniority is reversely related to premia: For Sample 1 constituents, the average senior unsecured CDS premium is 183 BPs while the average senior subordinated CDS premium is 243 BPs. Senior unsecured CDS premia are thus on average just 75.8% of senior subordinated CDS premia or 60 BPs lower. For Sample 2 constituents, the average LCDS premium is 309 BPs while the average senior unsecured CDS premium is 536 BPs. LCDS premia are thus on average just 58.1% of senior unsecured CDS premia or 227 BPs lower. For a breakdown of observations by firm, the reader is referred to Appendix B.

Interestingly, the average senior unsecured CDS premium is significantly higher for Sample 2 firms than for Sample 1 firms, the average difference being 353 BPs. There are three factors explaining this observation: First, ratings are slightly better for Sample 1 firms, as mentioned

[65] Remember that, by definition, leveraged loans are issued by sub-investment grade borrowers.

earlier. Second, more than 70% of observations in Sample 2 lie after the outbreak of the crisis in summer 2007, while this figure is less than 10% for Sample 1. Third, there is a systematic difference in the capital structure across samples. As it shall be seen below, this difference results in higher implied expected recovery rates for senior unsecured bonds in Sample 1 than in Sample 2, ceteris paribus.

	Sample 1 Constituents	Sample 2 Constituents
LCDSs	N/A	309 BPs
Senior Unsecured CDSs	183 BPs	536 BPs
Senior Subordinated CDSs	243 BPs	N/A
Ratio	75.8%	58.1%
Difference	60 BPs	227 BPs

Table 5.2: Overview of Average Premia
This table shows LCDS premia, senior unsecured CDS premia, senior subordinated CDS premia, ratios of premia (defined as s_{uns}/s_{sub} for Sample 1 constituents and as s_{loan}/s_{uns} for Sample 2 constituents), and differences of premia (defined as $s_{sub} - s_{uns}$ for Sample 1 constituents and as $s_{uns} - s_{loan}$ for Sample 2 constituents). Figures are averages over all firms and the entire observation period.

Figure 5.2 illustrates the evolution of average premia by type of debt. Shown are only the periods for which data for at least ten firms is available. Observable is a strong positive correlation of respective pairs and a sharp increase in premia since the outbreak of the crisis in summer 2007.

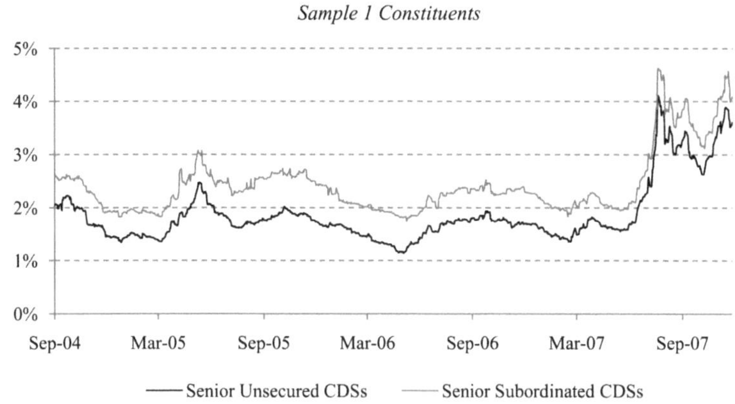

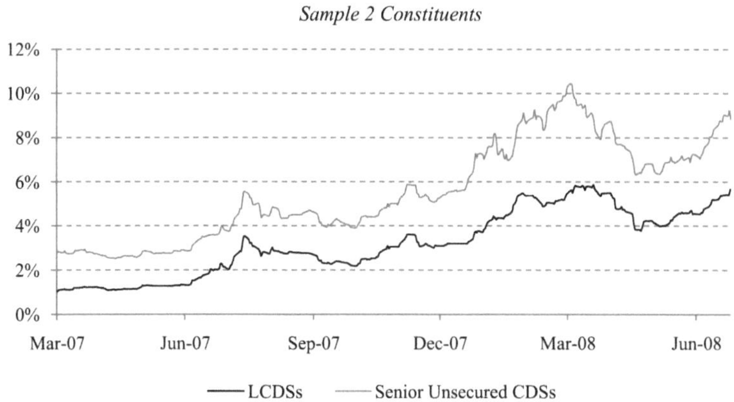

Figure 5.2: Evolution of Average Premia

This figure illustrates the evolution of senior unsecured CDS premia and senior subordinated CDS premia for Sample 1 constituents as well as LCDS premia and senior unsecured CDS premia for Sample 2 constituents. Figures are averages over all firms. Shown are only the respective periods for which data for at least ten firms is available.

5.1.3 Capital Structure Data

It was noted in Section 3.2 that instrument-specific recovery rates are a function of an issuer's capital structure at the time of default. Unfortunately, this variable is unobservable prior to such an event, and the capital structure at the initiation of the CDS is therefore used as an approximation. Based on the fiscal year-end financial statements of the firms in both samples, the percentage of senior secured loans, senior secured bonds, senior unsecured bonds, and senior subordinated bonds is identified for each firm. In senior secured loans, all secured term loans and secured revolving credit facilities are included. To provide a realistic estimate of the capital structure at default, undrawn revolving credit facilities are taken in, as well, as these are frequently triggered once a borrower faces financial distress. In senior unsecured bonds, all senior unsecured loans, bonds, and notes, as well as certain non-debt items that are generally treated as pari passu to senior unsecured debt are included. In particular, these are accounts payables, pension deficits in defined benefit schemes (i.e. projected benefit obligations less fair amount of plan assets) as well as operating and capital lease obligations. For each firm, this analysis is conducted at each fiscal year-end, starting with the fiscal year that precedes the year in which the first (L)CDS premium is observed and ending with the fiscal year in which the last premium is observed. Linear interpolation is then used to receive weekly figures.

Figure 5.3 illustrates the evolution of average capital structures by sample. In both samples, senior unsecured bonds are the most prevalent liability type, accounting on average for 59.3 and 55.7% of total liabilities in Sample 1 and 2, respectively. Senior secured loans constitute a substantial lot as well (26.1 and 36.9%). In Sample 1, their share has increased significantly over time, mostly at the expense of senior unsecured bonds. This may be due to the fact that ratings of Sample 1 firms have generally declined throughout the observation period, making senior secured loans more important a source of funding. The use of senior subordinated bonds is more prevalent in Sample 1 than in Sample 2 (14.1 and 4.4%). The share of senior secured bonds is negligible in both samples (0.6 and 3.1%).

These figures suggest that there is a systematic bias in capital structures: As all Sample 1 firms have liquidly-traded senior subordinated CDSs outstanding, it is likely that senior subordinated bonds play a major role in the financing efforts of these firms. The same argument applies to Sample 2 firms with respect to LCDSs and senior secured loans. This results in systematically different cushions for senior unsecured bonds: In Sample 1, on average 26.7% of liabilities are senior to senior unsecured bonds and 14.1% are junior. For Sample 2, these figures are 40.0 and 4.4%, respectively.

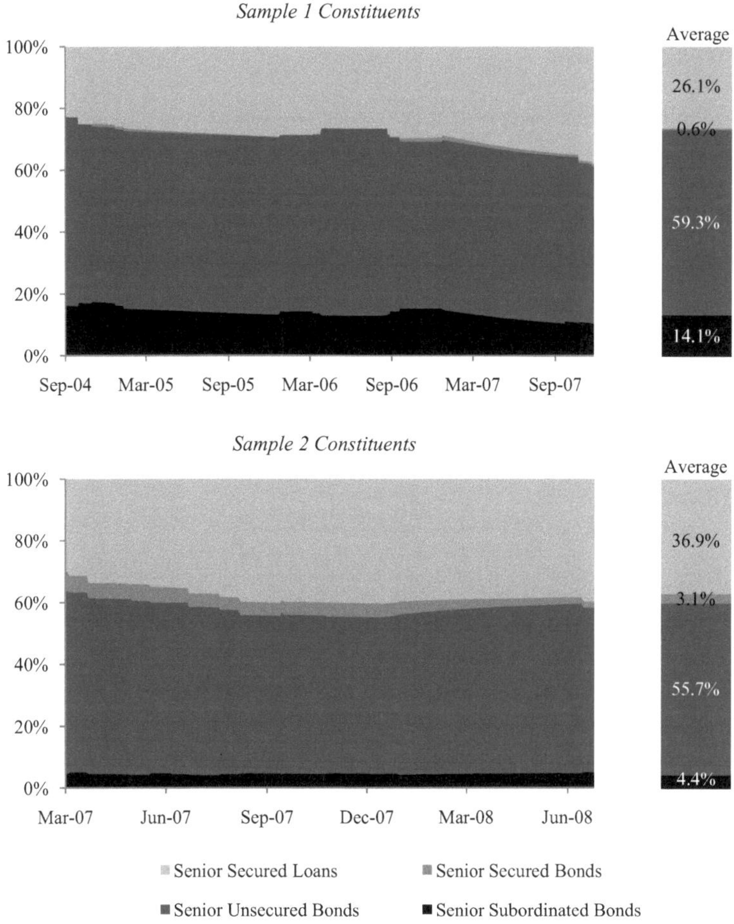

Figure 5.3. Evolution of Average Capital Structures

This figure illustrates the evolution of average capital structures, measured by the share that senior secured loans, senior secured bonds, senior unsecured bonds and loans, and senior subordinated bonds constitute of total liabilities. Shown are only the respective periods for which data for at least ten firms is available but averages comprise all data.

5.2 Empirical Specification

5.2.1 The Ratio of Premia

Having identified suitable pairs of (L)CDS premia now allows it to customize the generic approach presented in Chapter 3 to the data at hand. Let s_{loan}, s_{uns} and s_{sub} denote observed LCDS premia, senior unsecured CDS premia, and senior subordinated CDS premia, respectively. Equivalently to Eq. (3.8), ratios s_{uns}/s_{sub}, denoted by R_1 and s_{loan}/s_{uns}, denoted by R_2 are solely functions of the recovery rates of respective reference obligations, denoted by ρ_{loan}, ρ_{uns}, and ρ_{sub}:

$$R_1 = \frac{s_{uns}}{s_{sub}} = \frac{1 - E_t^{\tilde{Q}}\left[\rho_{uns} \,|1_{\{\tau \leq T\}} = 1\right]}{1 - E_t^{\tilde{Q}}\left[\rho_{sub} \,|1_{\{\tau \leq T\}} = 1\right]}, \tag{5.1}$$

$$R_2 = \frac{s_{loan}}{s_{uns}} = \frac{1 - E_t^{\tilde{Q}}\left[\rho_{loan} \,|1_{\{\tau \leq T\}} = 1\right]}{1 - E_t^{\tilde{Q}}\left[\rho_{uns} \,|1_{\{\tau \leq T\}} = 1\right]}. \tag{5.2}$$

Further, let $loan$, sec, uns, and sub denote the percentage share that senior secured loans, senior secured bonds, senior unsecured bonds, and senior subordinated bonds constitute of an issuer's total liabilities at the time of default. As no debt other than the mentioned is considered, it always holds that $loan + sec + uns + sub = 100\%$. Based on Eq. (3.10), the relations between instrument-specific recovery rates ρ_{loan}, ρ_{uns}, and ρ_{sub} and the ratio of firm value to liabilities at default is then given by:

$$\rho_{loan}(x) = \begin{cases} \dfrac{x}{loan} & x \in \,]0, a] \\ 1 & x \in \,]a, 1[\end{cases}, \tag{5.3}$$

$$\rho_{uns}(x) = \begin{cases} 0 & x \in \,]0, b] \\ \dfrac{x - b}{uns} & x \in \,]b, c] \\ 1 & x \in \,]c, 1[\end{cases}, \tag{5.4}$$

$$\rho_{sub}(x) = \begin{cases} 0 & x \in \,]0, c] \\ \dfrac{x - c}{sub} & x \in \,]c, 1[\end{cases} \tag{5.5}$$

for $x \in]0,1[$, where $a = loan$, $b = a + sec$, and $c = b + uns$.

Figure 5.4 illustrates this for a borrower with $loan = 30\%$, $sec = 5\%$, $uns = 55\%$, and $sub = 10\%$. If $0 < x < a = 30\%$, senior secured loan-holders recover only a fraction of their claims and bond-holders receive nothing. If $x \geq a$, senior secured loan-holders recover 100%. Holders of senior unsecured bonds receive proceeds if $x > b = 35\%$ and recover 100% if $x \geq c = 90\%$. For holders of senior subordinated bonds, the relevant barriers are 90 and 100%.

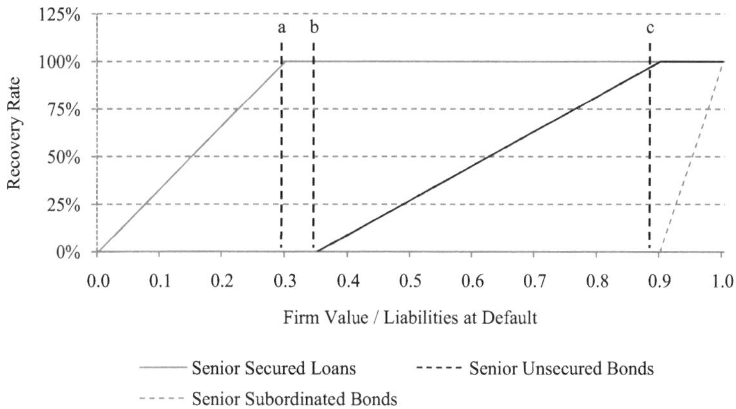

Figure 5.4: Illustrative Recovery Rates Given Default (II)
This figure illustrates the relationships between the ratio of firm value to liabilities at default and recovery rates for senior secured loans, senior unsecured bonds, and senior subordinated bonds. It is assumed that total liabilities consist of 30% senior secured loans, 5% senior secured bonds, 55% senior unsecured bonds, and 10% senior subordinated bonds and that the APR holds. Results are obtained using Eqs. (5.3) – (5.5).

Further, substituting Eqs. (5.3) – (5.5) into Eq. (3.11) gives formulas for implied expected instrument-specific recovery rates:

$$E_t^{\tilde{Q}}\left[\rho_{loan} \,|1_{\{\tau \leq T\}} = 1\right] = \int_0^a \frac{x}{loan} h_t(x)dx + \int_a^1 h_t(x)dx, \tag{5.6}$$

$$E_t^{\tilde{Q}}\left[\rho_{uns} \,|1_{\{\tau \leq T\}} = 1\right] = \int_b^c \frac{x-b}{uns} h_t(x)dx + \int_c^1 h_t(x)dx, \tag{5.7}$$

$$E_t^{\tilde{Q}}\left[\rho_{sub}\,|1_{\{\tau\leq T\}}=1\right]=\int_c^1\frac{x-c}{sub}h_t(x)dx. \tag{5.8}$$

Similarly, substituting Eqs. (5.3) – (5.5) into Eq. (3.12) gives formulas for the variance of respective recovery rates. These are shown in Appendix C.

To proceed with the empirical implementation of the model, a slight extension of notation is required. The CDS premia the analysis rests upon all refer to CDS contracts entered into as of the quote date with a maturity of five years. On the other hand, "seasoned" CDSs, i.e. instruments that have already been in existence for some time and thus have a shorter remaining life, are not considered. Therefore, let $s_{loan,t}$, $s_{uns,t}$, and $s_{sub,t}$ denote premia of CDSs initiated at time t that have a fixed maturity of five years and let $loan_t$, uns_t, and sub_t denote capital structure variables at that time. Substituting Eqs. (5.6) – (5.8) into Eqs. (5.1) and (5.2) then permits expressing model-implied ratios $s_{uns,t}/s_{sub,t}$, denoted by $\bar{R}_{1,t}$ and $s_{loan,t}/s_{uns,t}$, denoted by $\bar{R}_{2,t}$, as functions of the borrower's capital structure at time t and $h_t(x)$:

$$\bar{R}_{1,t}=\frac{s_{uns,t}}{s_{sub,t}}=\frac{1-\int_{b_t}^{c_t}\frac{(x-b_t)}{uns_t}h_t(x)dx-\int_{c_t}^{1}h_t(x)dx}{1-\int_{c_t}^{1}\frac{(x-c_t)}{sub_t}h_t(x)dx}, \tag{5.9}$$

$$\bar{R}_{2,t}=\frac{s_{loan,t}}{s_{uns,t}}=\frac{1-\int_{0}^{a_t}\frac{x}{loan_t}h_t(x)dx-\int_{a_t}^{1}h_t(x)dx}{1-\int_{b_t}^{c_t}\frac{(x-b_t)}{uns_t}h_t(x)dx-\int_{c_t}^{1}h_t(x)dx}. \tag{5.10}$$

Note that the only unknowns in Eqs. (5.9) and (5.10) are the mean μ_t and the standard deviation σ_t of $h_t(x)$ whereas all capital structure variables are known from firms' financial reports. Further, ratios $R_{1,t}$ and $R_{2,t}$ are observable in the market such that μ_t and σ_t can be estimated by calibrating ratios $\bar{R}$ to ratios R. To take into consideration firm- and industry-specific factors and general economic conditions in the calibration procedure, the next section continues with the empirical specification of μ_t and σ_t.

5.2.2 Linking the Implied Distribution to Economic Factors

It is likely that variables that explain historical recovery rates also drive implied recovery rates to some extent. Therefore, the mean of the implied probability distribution of recovery is defined as a function of some of the factors for which the discussion in Section 2.1 has shown that they are relevant for explaining historical recovery rates. In particular, the following four firm-specific factors are considered: i) *Financial leverage* (F_Lev), the ratio of long-term debt to total assets. High financial leverage implies that assets need to be shared among more debt-holders in the event of a default. Further, Acharya, Bharath, and Srinivasan (2007) argue that high leverage may be associated with a greater dispersion of ownership, resulting in more complex and lengthy resolution of bankruptcy proceedings.[66] Both effects should result in lower recovery rates in default; ii) *Asset tangibility* (F_Tan), the ratio of hard assets (proxied by property, plant, and equipment) to total assets. Cantor and Varma (2005) argue that firms with a high percentage of hard (i.e. likely to be revenue-producing and therefore more easily sellable) assets should achieve higher recovery rates in default; iii) *Interest coverage ratio* (F_IntCov), the ratio of EBITDA to interest expenses. Firms with high interest coverage dispose of assets that generate high earnings relative to interest expenses. In a default, a liquidation of these assets should result in higher recovery rates; and iv) *Quick ratio* (F_Quick), the ratio of current assets minus inventories to current liabilities. In a default, firms with a high quick ratio should be able to repay a higher share of their current liabilities out of their liquid current assets.

Further, three industry-specific factors suggested by Acharya, Bharath, and Srinivasan (2007) are employed: i) *Industry distress* (I_Diss), a dummy variable that takes the value one if the median 12-months stock return for the issuer's industry is less than -30%. Acharya et al. argue that industry distress is indicative of a downturn in the economic prospects of an industry and therefore associated with a reduction in the value of firms' assets and hence with lower recovery rates in default. They also test continuous, un-truncated industry equity returns but find that these do not possess explanatory power, suggesting that the effect of industry equity returns on recovery rates is essentially non-linear and restricted to situations where the industry is in distress; ii) *Industry illiquidity* (I_Illiq), the median inverse quick ratio of the issuer's industry;[67] and iii) *Industry financial leverage* (I_Lev), the median financial leverage of the issuer's industry. The latter two metrics are indicative of the financial condition of an issuer's peer firms. If this condition is delicate, the demand for the issuer's assets in the event of a default should be impaired, and recovery rates would suffer accordingly.

The industry of each firm is determined using three digit SIC codes, as reported in Appendix B. For each distinct code, the respective industry is then proxied by selecting the ten U.S. firms with the largest market capitalization that have the same SIC code. Accounting data for

66 However, Acharya et al. also note that in several occasions, highly leveraged transactions were particularly easily restructured.

67 Acharya et al. also implement an alternative definition of industry illiquidity, the median inverse interest coverage ratio, and obtain similar results.

firm- and industry-specific metrics are obtained from COMPUSTAT and companies' fiscal year-end financial statements (Form 10-K). Metrics are calculated based on fiscal year-end data and then interpolated to receive weekly figures.

	Count	Average	Stdev.	Min.	25th Percentile	Median	75th Percentile	Max.
F_Lev	5,229	0.531	0.712	0.046	0.280	0.403	0.583	6.408
F_Tan	5,229	0.355	0.216	0.009	0.217	0.358	0.522	0.803
F_IntCov	5,229	5.238	3.027	0.000	2.920	4.400	8.089	10.000
F_Quick	5,229	0.926	0.431	0.055	0.695	0.823	1.067	2.608
I_Diss	6,873	0.045	0.207	0.000	0.000	0.000	0.000	1.000
I_Illiq	7,585	1.025	0.519	0.186	0.722	0.970	1.235	5.403
I_Lev	7,861	0.247	0.141	0.000	0.145	0.220	0.327	0.716
CDX	394	1.498	0.636	0.686	1.048	1.237	1.777	3.963

Table 5.3: Overview of Explanatory Variables

This table shows summary statistics of the firm-specific, industry-specific, and macroeconomic factors that serve as explanatory variables for modeling the mean and the standard deviation of the implied probability distribution of recovery. Firm-specific factors are i) *Financial leverage* (F_Lev), the ratio of long-term debt to total assets, ii) *Asset tangibility* (F_Tan), the ratio of hard assets (proxied by property, plant, and equipment) to total assets, iii) *Interest coverage ratio* (F_IntCov), the ratio of EBITDA to interest expenses (for negative EBITDA (negative interest expenses) the interest coverage ratio is set to 0x (10x), otherwise, the ratio is capped at 10x), and iv) *Quick ratio* (F_Quick), the ratio of current assets minus inventories to current liabilities. Industry-specific factors are i) *Industry distress* (I_Diss), a dummy variable that takes the value one if the median 12-months stock return for the issuer's industry is less than -30%, ii) *Industry illiquidity* (I_Illiq), the median inverse quick ratio of the issuer's industry, and iii) *Industry financial leverage* (I_Lev), the median financial leverage of the issuer's industry. The *CDX High-Yield* (CDX), an index of CDS premia published by Markit that includes 100 equally-weighted, non-investment grade U.S. borrowers is chosen as macroeconomic factor. As the CDX is not available for the earlier years of the observation period, its initial set of constituents is used to extrapolate. The time series is scaled to 100% of its initial value. Accounting data for firm- and industry-specific metrics are obtained from COMPUSTAT and companies' fiscal year-end financial statements. Metrics are calculated based on fiscal year-end results and then interpolated to receive weekly figures.

Mentioned accounting metrics potentially capture differences that might exist between implied recovery rates of individual firms or industries. However, they are less qualified to signal the evolution of implied recovery rates over time. For that end, variables that reflect macroeconomic conditions are more apt. Therefore, the level of the *CDX High-Yield* (CDX), an index of CDS premia published by Markit that includes 100 equally-weighted, non-investment grade U.S. borrowers, is employed as final explanatory variable. If higher levels of the CDX imply higher recovery risk, they should be associated with lower implied recovery rates. GDP growth and S&P 500 returns, two other macroeconomic indicators that have proved useful for explaining historical recovery rates are, however, not included. GDP data is available on a quarterly basis only which conflicts with the relative brevity of observation periods. Equity returns are indirectly factored in through the proxies for industry distress.

Table 5.3 shows summary statistics for all explanatory variables. The average industry-specific financial leverage is 24.7% while this figure is 53.1% for firms in Sample 1 and 2 which, as mentioned earlier, almost all have a sub-investment grade rating. Average asset tangibility is 35.5%. The interest coverage ratio is set to 0x (10x) for negative EBITDA (negative interest expenses) and otherwise is capped at 10x. The resulting average is 5.2x. The average quick ratio is 92.6%. The dummy variable for industry distress takes the value of one in 4.5% of cases. The average of the median inverse quick ratio, used as an indicator for industry illiquidity, is 102.5%. The CDX is scaled to 100% of its initial value and fluctuates between 68.6 and 396.3% of that figure.

In summary, the mean μ of the implied probability distribution of recovery at time t and for firm n is given by:

$$\begin{aligned}\mu_{t,n} = \beta_0 + \beta_1 F\_Lev_{t,n} + \beta_2 F\_Tan_{t,n} + \beta_3 F\_IntCov_{t,n} + \beta_4 F\_Quick_{t,n} \\ + \beta_5 I\_Diss_{t,n} + \beta_6 I\_Illiq_{t,n} + \beta_7 I\_Lev_{t,n} + \beta_8 CDX_t\end{aligned} \tag{5.11}$$

where $\beta_0, \ldots, \beta_8$ are constant parameters.

There is no theoretical reason why the standard deviation of implied recovery rates should be constant over time. Rather, it might be higher in times of high uncertainty and vice versa. To account for this, the standard deviation is modeled as a function of the CDX. If higher levels of the CDX are indicative of higher uncertainty, they should be associated with a higher standard deviation. This approach is, however, complicated by the fact that the first two moments of the beta distribution are related, as mentioned earlier. For instance, a particular standard deviation can be relatively high or even unattainable if the mean of the implied probability distribution of recovery is, say, very low. On the other hand, it can be relatively low if the mean is close to 50%. Therefore, instead of modeling the absolute standard deviation directly, the excess standard deviation over the minimum standard deviation for a given mean, denoted by $\sigma_{prem,t}$, is employed, having the nice property that it always lies in the unit interval. Using Eq. (3.17) and remembering from Eq. (3.18) that $\sigma_{inf} = 0$, the absolute standard deviation at time t and for firm n is then given by:

$$\sigma_{t,n} = \left(\sigma_{sup,t,n} - \sigma_{inf,t,n}\right) \sigma_{prem,t} + \sigma_{inf,t,n} \tag{5.12}$$

$$= \sigma_{sup,t,n}\, \sigma_{prem,t} \quad \sigma_{prem,t} \in]0,1[$$

where:

$$\sigma_{prem,t} = \gamma_0 + \gamma_1 CDX_t \tag{5.13}$$

and γ_0, γ_1 are constant parameters. Thus, being a function only of the CDX, $\sigma_{prem,t}$ is identical for all firms, whereas $\sigma_{t,n}$ additionally depends on the mean of the implied probability distribution of recovery through $\sigma_{sup,t,n} = \sqrt{\mu_{t,n} - \mu_{t,n}{}^2}$ and therefore is firm-specific.

5.2.3 Calibration Results

With the mean and the standard deviation of the implied distribution of recovery being specified by Eqs. (5.11) and (5.12), the model-implied ratios $\bar{R}_{1,t,n}$ and $\bar{R}_{2,t,n}$ are functions of time-dependent firm-specific capital structure variables, time-dependent firm- and industry-specific accounting metrics, the level of the CDX, and unknown, time-invariant parameters $\gamma_0, \gamma_1, \beta_0, \dots, \beta_8$. The latter are estimated by minimizing the sum of squared differences between actual and model-implied ratios over the entire observation period and over all I firms in Sample 1 and all J firms in Sample 2:

$$RMSE = \min_{\gamma_0,\gamma_1,\beta_0,\dots,\beta_8} \sqrt{\frac{\sum_{n=1}^{I}\sum_{t=1}^{T_n}\left(R_{1,t,n} - \bar{R}_{1,t,n}\right)^2 + \sum_{n=I+1}^{I+J}\sum_{t=1}^{T_n}\left(R_{2,t,n} - \bar{R}_{2,t,n}\right)^2}{\sum_{n=1}^{I+J} T_n}} \tag{5.14}$$

where T_n denotes the number of observations for firm n.

Due to the nonlinearity of Eq. (5.14), the significance of explanatory variables cannot be determined without further ado. Therefore, a two-step estimation procedure is applied: First, based on estimates for γ_0 and γ_1 (resulting in given $\sigma_{prem,t}$), means $\tilde{\mu}_{t,n}$ are chosen such that model-implied ratios are equal to actual ratios for each firm and at each point in time, i.e. $\bar{R}_{1,t,n} = R_{1,t,n}$ if firm n belongs to Sample 1 and $\bar{R}_{2,t,n} = R_{2,t,n}$ if it belongs to Sample 2. Since explanatory variables $F\_Lev_{t,n}, F\_Tan_{t,n}, \dots, CDX_t$ are linearly related to $\tilde{\mu}_{t,n}$, standard errors for parameters $\beta_0, \dots, \beta_8$ can be determined in a straightforward manner, conditional on estimates for γ_0 and γ_1. Second, given estimates for $\beta_0, \dots, \beta_8$ (resulting in given $\mu_{t,n}$), excess standard deviations $\tilde{\sigma}_{prem,t}$ are chosen such that the squared difference between model-implied ratios and actual ratios is minimized for each firm and at each point in time, i.e. $\min_{\gamma_0,\gamma_1}\left(R_{1,t,n} - \bar{R}_{1,t,n}\right)^2$ if firm n belongs to Sample 1 and $\min_{\gamma_0,\gamma_1}\left(R_{2,t,n} - \bar{R}_{2,t,n}\right)^2$ if it belongs to Sample 2. Note that this difference generally is not exactly zero because $\tilde{\sigma}_{prem,t}$ is not firm-specific. Since the explanatory variable CDX_t is linearly related to $\tilde{\sigma}_{prem,t}$, standard errors for parameters γ_0 and γ_1 can again be determined in a straightforward manner, this time conditional on estimates for $\beta_0, \ldots, \beta_8$.

Table 5.4 shows estimation results for parameters $\gamma_0, \gamma_1, \beta_0, \ldots, \beta_8$ and associated standard errors. Signs of coefficients are as expected and in accordance with research on the determinants of physical recovery rates: Financial leverage (both, firm- and industry-specific), industry illiquidity, industry distress, and the CDX are negatively related to the mean of the implied probability distribution. For instance, if an industry is in distress or the level of the CDX doubles, implied expected firm-wide recovery rates decrease 2.6 and 3.1% on average, ceteris paribus. Asset tangibility, interest coverage, and the quick ratio, on the other hand, are positively related to the mean. Further, the CDX is positively related to the excess standard deviation $(\sigma_{prem,t})$. Due to the interrelation of μ and σ discussed earlier, this does, however, not imply that the absolute standard deviation must always increase if the CDX decreases. The evolution of the absolute standard deviation over time is examined in Section 5.3.3.

	β_0	β_1 (F_Lev)	β_2 (F_Tan)	β_3 (F_IntCov)	β_4 (F_Quick)	β_5 (I_Diss)	β_6 (I_Illiq)	β_7 (I_Lev)	β_8 (CDX)
Coeff.	0.3557***	-0.0101**	0.0031	0.0052***	0.0298***	-0.0257**	-0.0214***	-0.0217	-0.0312***
Std. Err.	0.0162	0.0043	0.0152	0.0011	0.0066	0.0119	0.0069	0.0176	0.0057

	γ_0	γ_1 (CDX)							
Coeff.	0.6308***	0.0431***							
Std. Err.	0.0106	0.0073				RMSE	0.137	Adj. R^2	0.330

Table 5.4: Estimation Results for the Implied Distribution of Recovery

This table shows estimation results for the implied probability distribution of recovery. It is assumed that implied recovery rates follow a beta distribution. The mean of this distribution is modelled as a function of financial leverage (F_Lev), asset tangibility (F_Tan), the interest coverage ratio (F_IntCov), the quick ratio (F_Quick), industry distress (I_Diss), industry illiquidity (I_Illiq), industry financial leverage (I_Lev), and the CDX (Eq. (5.11)). The excess standard deviation of the distribution is modelled as a function of the CDX (Eq. (5.13)). Standard errors for $\beta_0, \ldots, \beta_8$ are conditional on estimates of γ_0, γ_1 and vice versa. *** and ** indicate significance at the 1 and 5% confidence level, respectively. The RMSE is obtained using Eq. (5.14).

With the exception of asset tangibility and industry-specific financial leverage, all coefficients are significant at the 5% confidence level or higher. The RMSE is 0.137 and the adjusted R^2 is

0.330, indicating that the explanatory variables fail to capture some of the week-to-week variation in observed ratios.

The model achieves a much higher explanatory power when it comes to explaining the general level of actual ratios as opposed to their week-to-week variation. To see this, firms' model-implied ratios, averaged over the respective observation period (independent variable), are compared to average actual ratios (dependent variable). As Figure 5.5 illustrates, pairs of ratios lie close to the 45-degree line, one exception being the pair for Freeport McMoran. If Freeport is disregarded, the hypothesis that the ordinary least squares line has an intercept equal to zero and a slope equal to one cannot be rejected at the 10% confidence level. The adjusted R^2 is 0.816.

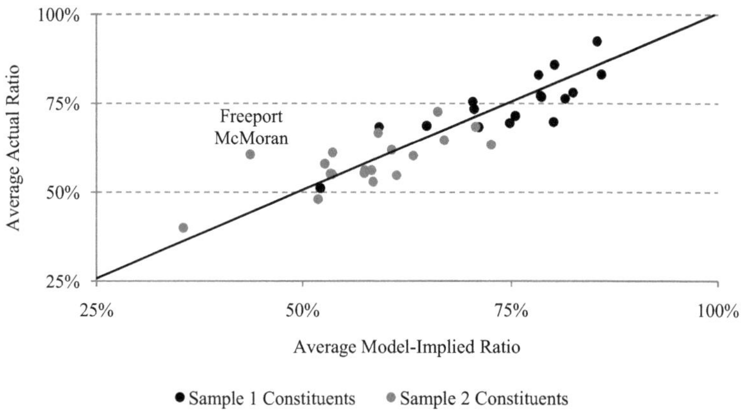

Figure 5.5: Average Model-Implied vs. Average Actual Ratios
This figure illustrates the relation of average model-implied ratios and average observed ratios. Figures are averages over the respective observation period.

5.3 Estimation Results of Market-Implied Recovery Rates

5.3.1 Implied Firm-Wide and Instrument-Specific Recovery Rates

Based on estimated model parameters $\gamma_0, \gamma_1, \beta_0, \ldots, \beta_8$ and issuers' capital structure data, it is now straightforward to calculate implied expected firm-wide and instrument-specific recovery rates and the standard deviation of implied recovery rates for each firm and for each week. Appendix D lists results for each firm, averaged over the respective observation period and Table 5.5 further aggregates figures over all firms. The average implied expected firm-wide recovery rate is 33.4%. Maximum and minimum results vary notably, mostly due to observation periods differing from firm to firm[68], but firm- and industry-specific factors are of relevance, as well.

	Firm-Wide	Senior Secured Loans	Senior Unsecured Bonds	Senior Subordinated Bonds
Implied Expected Recovery Rate				
Average	33.4%	53.7%	24.0%	5.8%
Median	33.3%	53.4%	22.8%	4.7%
Max.	41.0%	75.7%	42.9%	11.2%
Min.	22.7%	36.3%	10.0%	1.4%
Avg. Standard Deviation of Implied Rec. Rates	32.5%	41.4%	34.3%	18.4%

Table 5.5: Implied Firm-Wide and Instrument-Specific Recovery Rates
This table shows average, median, maximum, and minimum implied expected recovery rates for the entire firm, senior secured loans, senior unsecured bonds, and senior subordinated bonds as well as average standard deviations of respective recovery rates. Estimates of implied expected recovery rates are obtained using Eqs. (3.14) and (5.6) – (5.8). Estimates of the standard deviation of implied recovery rates are obtained using Eqs. (3.15) and (C.i) – (C.iii). The estimation approach is specified by Eqs. (5.14).

Cantor, Emery, and Stumpp (2006) find that the dispersion of historically realized ratios of firm value to liabilities at default is well-described by a beta distribution that is restricted to [0,1.2] with an average firm-wide recovery rate of 50% and a standard deviation of 26%. It is insightful to visualize the density of this distribution and to compare it to the implied density of firm-wide recovery. The latter is constructed from the average implied expected firm-wide recovery rate (33.4%) and the average standard deviation of implied firm-wide recovery rates (32.5%). Figure 5.6 illustrates that while the physical density is bell-shaped, the implied density is approximately U-shaped (due to its higher standard deviation) with much of the probability mass concentrating at the lower bound.

This indicates that ex ante there is high uncertainty as to how much borrowers will recover, should a default occur. This finding does not come at much of a surprise: Several studies on historical recovery rates show that a substantial share of their variation remains unexplained, even when a broad range of issue-, firm-, and industry-specific factors as well as macroeco-

[68] For instance, observations for Solectron (average firm-wide recovery rate: 41.0%) all lie prior to the outbreak of the credit crisis in July 2007 whereas observations for MichaelStores (average firm-wide recovery rate: 22.7%) all lie thereafter. The evolution of implied expected recovery rates over time is examined in Section 5.3.3.

nomic indicators are employed as explanatory variables[69], and Cantor, Emery, and Stumpp (2006) observe that "it is extremely difficult to predict firm-wide loss given default rates well in advance of default". Further, it is noteworthy that the mean of the implied distribution is much lower than that of its physical counterpart. This suggests that investors require a premium for taking recovery risk, a topic examined more closely later in this chapter.

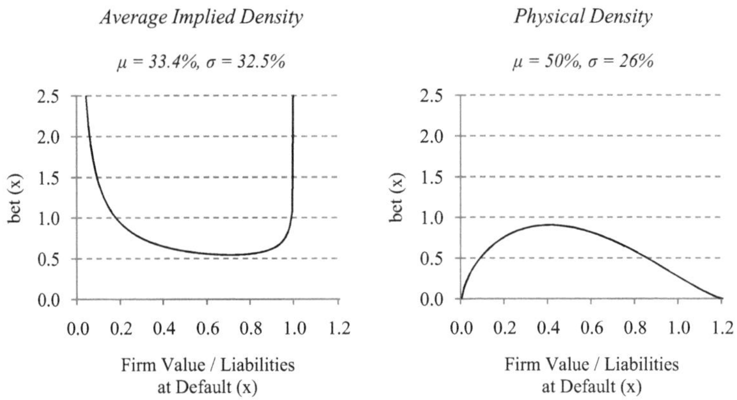

Figure 5.6: Physical vs. Average Implied Densities of Recovery
This figure illustrates the shape of the implied probability density of recovery rates, obtained by averaging over all firms and the entire observation period. Also shown is the probability density of historically observed ratios of firm value to liabilities at default (Cantor, Emery, and Stumpp (2006)), taken as a proxy for the physical density of firm-wide recovery rates. In both cases, it is assumed that recovery rates follow a beta distribution.

It was mentioned in Section 2.1 that seniority is the predominant driver of recovery in default, with average physical recovery rates being 66% for senior secured loans, 40% for senior unsecured bonds, and 32% for senior subordinated loans. Table 5.5 shows that seniority is similarly important a characteristic for *implied* instrument-specific recovery rates, average estimates being 53.7, 24.0, and 5.8%, respectively. Again, implied figures are thus significantly below historical averages, further substantiating the hypothesis that there is a risk premium in implied recovery rates. It is, however, striking that the gap is particularly large for senior subordinated bonds (physical: 32%, implied: 5.8%), both in absolute as well as in relative terms. In Section 5.4.2 it is shown that this is due to the extraordinarily high standard deviation of physical senior subordinated recovery rates.

[69] Depending on regression model specifications, R^2s obtained by some of these studies are: Keisman, Van de Castle, and Yang (2000): 37 – 48%, Covitz and Han (2004): 33 – 44%, Cantor and Varma (2005): 53 – 59%, Chava, Stefanescu, and Turnbull (2006): 12 – 27%, Acharya, Bharath, and Srinivasan (2007): 51 – 68%.

Estimates of instrument-specific recovery rates vary widely across firms, too (36.3 to 75.7% for senior secured loans, 10.0 to 42.9% for senior unsecured bonds, 1.4 to 11.2% for senior subordinated bonds). Part of this variation is due to the same factors that drive variation in firm-specific recovery rates (i.e. firm- and industry specific explanatory variables, different observation periods). For instrument-specific recovery rates, differences in issuers' capital structure are, however, a major driver as well, as the next section shows.

5.3.2 The Impact of Debt Cushion

Most studies on the link between asset quality and recovery in default rely on dummy variables for seniority to indirectly proxy debt cushion effects.[70] This approach, however, comes at the disadvantage of not being able to capture the variation in recovery rates *within* a particular type of debt, and as was shown earlier, this variation can be substantial. A more thorough exploration of this matter is therefore in order.

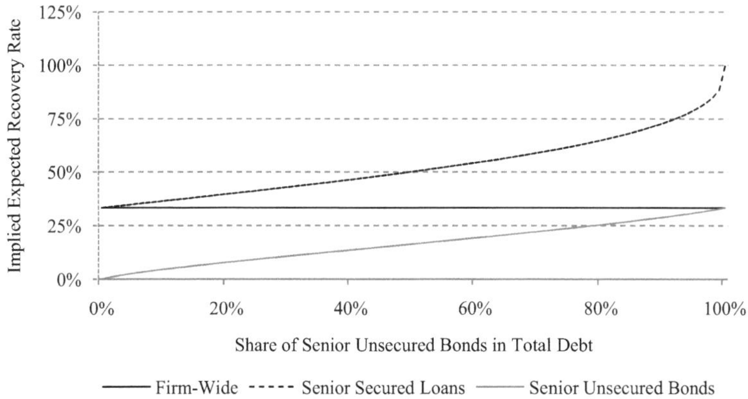

Figure 5.7: Recovery in Default and Capital Structure
This figure illustrates the impact of capital structure on implied expected recovery rates of senior secured loans and senior unsecured bonds. The example supposes a firm with an implied probability distribution of recovery with $\mu = 33.4\%$ and $\sigma = 32.5\%$ that has outstanding only senior secured loans and senior unsecured bonds.

[70] One exception is Cantor and Varma (2005) who use debt cushion below to explain historically observed recovery rates. They find that issues with more than 60% debt cushion below recover about 76% more than issues with less than 15% debt cushion below.

For a given implied distribution of firm-wide recovery rates, the theoretical impact of capital structure (as measured by debt cushion above and below) on instrument-specific recovery rates can be easily deduced using Eqs. (5.6) – (5.8). Figure 5.7 illustrates this for a hypothetical firm that has outstanding only senior secured loans and senior unsecured bonds (i.e. $loan + uns = 100\%$), the implied probability distribution of recovery being given by $\mu = 33.4\%$ and $\sigma = 32.5\%$. For $uns = 0\%$, it holds that $E^{\tilde{Q}}\left[\rho_{loan} | 1_{\{\tau \leq T\}} = 1\right] = E^{\tilde{Q}}\left[\rho_{firm} | 1_{\{\tau \leq T\}} = 1\right] = \mu$. As the share of senior unsecured bonds increases, senior secured loans benefit from more debt cushion below such that $\lim_{uns \to 100\%} E^{\tilde{Q}}\left[\rho_{loan} | 1_{\{\tau \leq T\}} = 1\right] = 100\%$. Similarly, the recovery rate of senior unsecured bonds approaches the firm-wide recovery rate as the share of senior secured loans approaches zero, i.e. $\lim_{loan \to 0\%} E^{\tilde{Q}}\left[\rho_{uns} | 1_{\{\tau \leq T\}} = 1\right] = \mu$.

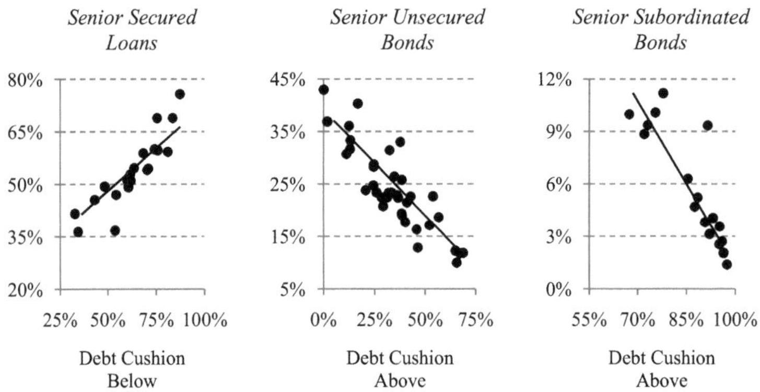

Figure 5.8: The Impact of Debt Cushion
This figure illustrates the impact of capital structure (as measured by debt cushion below and debt cushion above) on implied expected recovery rates of senior secured loans, senior unsecured bonds, and senior subordinated bonds (y-axes). Figures are averages over the respective observation period.

Considering, though, that implied distributions are not only different for each firm but also change over time, it is expedient to examine the *average* relation of instrument-specific recovery rates and issuers' capital structure, as implied by estimation results. Figure 5.8 illustrates that for senior secured loans, a one percentage point increase in debt cushion below is on average associated with a 0.60 percentage point increase in recovery rates, the adjusted R^2 being 0.758. For senior unsecured bonds (senior subordinated bonds), an increase in debt cushion above of the same magnitude is on average associated with a 0.40 (0.29) percentage point decrease, the adjusted R^2s being 0.749 and 0.736.[71] This implies that issuers' capital structure is responsible for most of the tremendous variation in recovery rates within a particular type of debt. Of course, these figures are only approximate because the true relationships are not linear, as Figure 5.7 showed.

5.3.3 The Impact of Changes in the Economic Environment

The discussion in Section 2.1 showed that physical recovery rates exhibit substantial co-movement with factors that are related to the business cycle such as GDP growth, equity returns, and economic indices. Rösch and Scheule (2005) find that senior unsecured bonds recovered only around 40% in 1990 and 30% in 2000 – 2002, years in which many economies fared badly. By contrast, this figure was approximately 50% for the time in between. Covitz and Han (2004), Düllmann and Trapp (2004), Harpaintner, Rachev, and Trück (2005), and Bruche and Gonzáles-Aguado (2009) obtain comparable results, and there is little reason why a similar behavior should not be observable under the pricing measure.

Figure 5.9 illustrates the evolution of the average implied expected firm-wide recovery rate and the average standard deviation of implied firm-wide recovery rates over the entire observation period. Between early 2001 and autumn 2002, a time that saw the burst of the internet bubble, 9/11, and various accounting scandals (Enron, WorldCom, and Tyco, to name but a few), recovery rates plunged by more than 12 percentage points from 33.8 to 21.6%. Until year-end 2004, however, they recovered to what could be called their "non-crisis-level" (approximately 35%) and stayed there for the three years to come. Around July 2007 when the distortions in the U.S. sub-prime mortgage market unveiled for the first time, recovery rates started to deteriorate again and fell to below 30% at the end of the observation period.

The standard deviation of implied firm-wide recovery rates fluctuates only moderately and does not leave the band of 31.8 to 33.8%. Observable is a jump subsequent to 9/11, generally higher values between autumn 2002 and autumn 2003, and an increase since July 2007. This is despite the simultaneous drop of expected recovery rates, meaning that the excess standard deviation over the minimum standard deviation (not shown) is extremely sensitive to distress. This suggests that in uncertain times, investors not only reduce their estimates of recovery given default, but are also aware that their predictions may have become less reliable.

[71] The relation of debt cushion below and recovery rates of senior unsecured bonds (not shown) is positive but less clear cut. This is due to debt cushion above being the dominant driver for this type of debt.

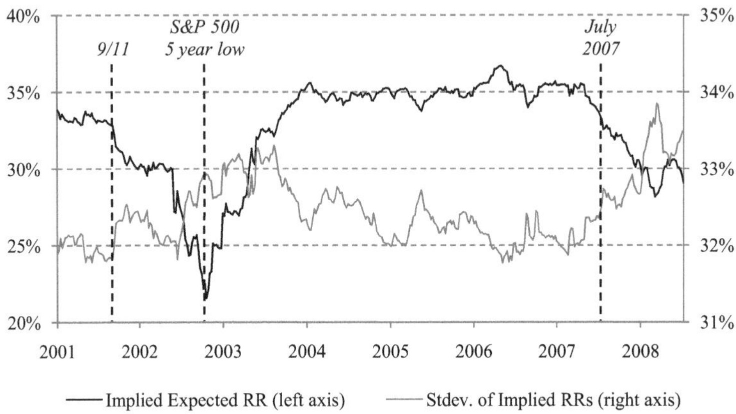

Figure 5.9: Evolution of Implied Firm-Wide Recovery Rates
This figure illustrates the evolution of implied expected firm-wide recovery rates and the standard deviation of implied firm-wide recovery rates. Figures are averages over all firms.

5.3.4 The Relation to Ratings

Historical evidence as to whether credit ratings are indicative of recovery given default is mixed: Emery (2007) studies the relation of Moody's corporate family ratings and historical firm-wide recovery rates. Corporate family ratings mainly convey information as to an issuer's general default risk, rather than specifically accounting for the risk associated with a particular debt instrument. His results suggest that there is no systematic link between the two, from which it follows that higher default risk is not necessarily associated with lower default-conditional recovery. Altman, Resti, and Sironi (2004), on the other hand, examine the link between Moody's instrument-specific ratings and historical instrument-specific recovery rates. In addition to default risk, instrument-specific ratings take capital structure and collateral quality into consideration and thus account specifically for the recovery prospects of a particular debt issue. Consistent with intuition, Altman et al. find that bonds with an investment grade rating recover a substantially higher fraction than those with a sub-investment grade rating.

To see whether these relations persist for implied figures, the average implied expected firm-wide recovery rates for firms with the same Moody's corporate family rating as well as the average implied expected instrument-specific recovery rates for debt instruments with the same Moody's instrument-specific credit rating are calculated. Table 5.6 shows that the average firm-wide recovery rate is 35.7% for Baa-rated firms and only slightly lower for Ba- and B-rated firm (33.4 and 32.7%). Using standard statistical tests, the null hypothesis of no relation between corporate family ratings and firm-wide recovery rates cannot be rejected at the 10% confidence level, a result analogous to that of Emery.[72] Instrument-specific ratings, on the other hand, seem to qualify as indicators for recovery prospects: Average instrument-specific recovery rates range from as high as 45.0% for Baa-rated debt to as low as 16.1% for Caa-rated debt. The null hypothesis of no relation can be rejected at the 1% confidence level, confirming results of Altman et al., too.

	Baa	Ba	B	Caa
Firm-wide	35.7%	33.4%	32.7%	NA
Count	2	17	15	0
Instrument-specific	45.0%	36.4%	21.1%	16.1%
Count	9	27	21	8

Table 5.6: Implied Expected Recovery Rates by Moody's Rating
This table shows average implied expected firm-wide recovery rates for firms with the same corporate family rating and average implied expected instrument-specific recovery rates for debt with the same instrument-specific credit rating. Ratings are as published by Moody's and obtained from Bloomberg. In each case, the average rating during the observation period is used. "Count" indicates the number of firms/issues with a particular rating.

As mentioned, corporate family as well as instrument-specific ratings reflect issuers' default risk, albeit not necessarily solely. However, rating agencies also derive pure estimates of default-conditional recovery rates for debt instruments of a particular seniority. These recovery estimates are based on an analysis of priority of claims and the distribution of *historical* recovery rates and, thus, should not comprise a premium for recovery risk.[73]

Figure 5.10 illustrates that there is a strong relation between estimated implied-expected instrument-specific recovery rates and Moody's recovery point estimates for the same instruments, the adjusted R^2 being 80.2%. With the exception of Univision and Visteon, observations lie within or close to the "region of risk premia" (i.e. below the 45-degree line), meaning that Moody's estimates of (physical) recovery are greater than implied estimates. The slope of the ordinary least squares line is 0.632, significant at the 1% confidence level, whereas the intercept is not significantly different from zero. These results show that the employed approach to prioritizing claims produces results similar to those of Moody's and that investors require a substantial premium for taking recovery risk.

72 Statistical tests are performed using all rating notches and not just full letter designations.
73 Solomon (2006) describes Moody's approach to deriving recovery estimates. S&P and Fitch apply similar methodologies.

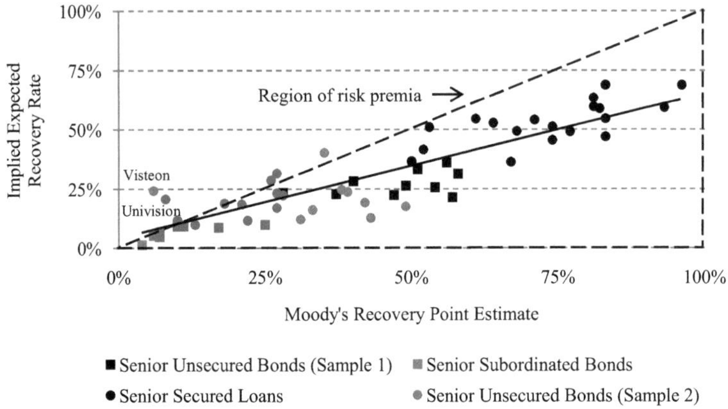

Figure 5.10: Implied Expected Recovery Rates vs. Moody's Recovery Point Estimates
This figure illustrates the relation of Moody's recovery point estimates (as of June 2008 and where available) and implied expected instrument-specific recovery rates, averaged over the respective observation period.

5.4 Robustness

5.4.1 Alternative Parameterization

To assure that estimates of implied recovery are robust with regard to the chosen functional form of the implied probability distribution of recovery $h_t(x)$, the model is re-estimated based on an alternative parameterization. Following Güntay, Madan, and Unal (2003), Düllmann and Trapp (2004), and Rösch and Scheule (2005), it is assumed that the ratio of firm value to total liabilities at default x is related to a normally distributed variable y with mean $\bar{\mu}_t$ and variance $\bar{\sigma}_t{}^2$ by the logit transformation $x = e^y/(1+e^y)$.[74] x then follows the transformed normal density:

$$t_t(x) = \frac{1}{\sqrt{2\pi}\bar{\sigma}_t x(1-x)} exp\left(-\frac{\left(log\left(\frac{x}{1-x}\right)-\bar{\mu}_t\right)^2}{2\bar{\sigma}_t{}^2}\right) \quad x \in]0,1[. \tag{5.15}$$

[74] Güntay et al. use this assumption for their estimation of implied recovery rates, Düllmann and Trapp and Rösch and Scheule analyze the determinants of historical recovery rates.

Similar to the beta distribution, the transformed normal distribution is fully specified by its first two moments, can assume U- as well as bell shapes, and is capable of reproducing all combinations of mean and standard deviation that are theoretically conceivable for a probability density with support in the unit interval.[75]

	β_0	β_1 (F_Lev)	β_2 (F_Tan)	β_3 (F_IntCov)	β_4 (F_Quick)	β_5 (I_Diss)	β_6 (I_Illiq)	β_7 (I_Lev)	β_8 (CDX)
Coeff.	0.3551***	-0.0081*	0.0059	0.0054***	0.0329***	-0.0243**	-0.0174**	-0.0214	-0.0251***
Std. Err.	0.0162	0.0042	0.0151	0.0011	0.0066	0.0119	0.0069	0.0175	0.0057

	γ_0	γ_1 (CDX)							
Coeff.	0.6404***	0.0404***							
Std. Err.	0.0107	0.0074				RMSE	0.138	Adj. R^2	0.327

Table 5.7: Estimation Results for the Transformed Normal Distribution

This table shows estimation results for the implied probability distribution of recovery. It is assumed that implied recovery rates follow a transformed normal distribution. The mean of this distribution is modelled as a function of financial leverage (F_Lev), asset tangibility (F_Tan), interest coverage ratio (F_IntCov), quick ratio (F_Quick), industry distress (I_Diss), industry illiquidity (I_Illiq), industry financial leverage (I_Lev), and the CDX (Eq. (5.11)). The excess standard deviation of the distribution is modelled as a function of the CDX (Eq. (5.13)). Standard errors for $\beta_0, \dots, \beta_8$ are conditional on estimates of γ_0, γ_1 and vice versa. ***, **, and * indicate significance at the 1, 5, and 10% confidence level, respectively. The RMSE is obtained using Eq. (5.14).

Table 5.7 shows estimation results obtained for the transformed normal distribution. Without exception, signs of coefficients are identical to those presented earlier for the beta distribution (Table 5.4). Confidence levels, the size of coefficients, the RMSE, and the adjusted R^2 are very similar, too and for practical purposes can be considered identical. The resulting average implied expected firm-wide recovery rate is 35.2% and the average standard deviation of implied recovery rates is 33.2% (not shown). Again, these figures are not markedly different from results for the beta distribution (33.4 and 32.5%, respectively). Further, the central finding that the implied density of recovery is U-shaped persists for the transformed normal distribution.[76] This suggests that estimation results are robust for different parameterizations of $h_t(x)$.

[75] Appendix A.II shows the supremum and infimum of the standard deviation of this distribution for a given mean.

[76] To confirm that the observed U-shape is not an artifact of the mathematical properties of the beta and the transformed normal distribution, the model is re-estimated based on a third parameterization of $h_t(x)$, given by the quadratic density function:

5.4.2 Sample-Specific Calibration

All recovery estimates discussed hitherto where obtained by calibrating parameters $\gamma_0, \gamma_1, \beta_0, \dots, \beta_8$ over all firms in Sample 1 and 2 at the same time, and it is of interest to see whether results are similar if the model is re-calibrated for both samples separately. If this were not the case, one would have to suppose that factors such as LCDS cancellation or differences in the liquidity of LCDSs and CDSs have a significant impact on estimation results, contrary to expectations.

To carry out a sample-specific estimation, Eq. (5.14) is split into:

$$RMSE_1 = \min_{\gamma_0,\gamma_1,\beta_0,\dots,\beta_8} \sqrt{\frac{\sum_{n=1}^{I} \sum_{t=1}^{T_n} \left(R_{1,t,n} - \bar{R}_{1,t,n}\right)^2}{\sum_{n=1}^{I} T_n}} \tag{5.16}$$

for Sample 1 firms and:

$$RMSE_2 = \min_{\gamma_0,\gamma_1,\beta_0,\dots,\beta_8} \sqrt{\frac{\sum_{n=I+1}^{I+J} \sum_{t=1}^{T_n} \left(R_{2,t,n} - \bar{R}_{2,t,n}\right)^2}{\sum_{n=I+1}^{I+J} T_n}} \tag{5.17}$$

for Sample 2 firms.

Table 5.8 shows resulting estimates for firm-wide and instrument-specific recovery rates as well as for the standard deviation of implied recovery rates. Comparing these to corresponding figures for the joint estimation (Table 5.5) shows that results come out slightly lower, although deviations are very limited: The average recovery rate is 32.6% firm-wide (joint estimation: 33.4%), 51.8% for senior secured loans (53.7%), 22.6% for senior unsecured bonds (24.0%), and 4.0% for senior subordinated bonds (5.8%). Standard deviations come out slightly lower as well, which is due to their relation to recovery rates. On the level of the individual firm, estimates are not markedly different either, as Appendix E shows. This indicates that results are robust with regard to the chosen calibration procedure.

$$u_t(x) = a_{0,t} + a_{1,t}\left(x - \frac{1}{2}\right) + a_{2,t}\left(x - \frac{1}{2}\right)^2$$

with $\int_0^1 u_t(x)\,dx = 1$ and $u_t(x) \geq 0$ for all $x \in [0,1]$ where $\alpha_{0,t}$, $\alpha_{1,t}$ and $\alpha_{2,t}$ are shape parameters. Appendix A.III shows the maximum and minimum of the standard deviation of this distribution for a given mean. Again, the resulting implied density is found to be U-shaped.

	Firm-wide	Senior Secured Loans	Senior Unsecured Bonds	Senior Subordinated Bonds
Implied Expected Recovery Rate				
Average	32.6%	51.8%	22.6%	4.0%
Median	32.2%	49.6%	21.6%	2.8%
Max.	43.4%	75.0%	45.5%	9.3%
Min.	23.7%	36.1%	9.0%	0.4%
Avg. Standard Deviation of Implied Rec. Rates	30.8%	41.3%	32.5%	14.4%

Table 5.8: Implied Recovery Rates for Sample-Specific Calibration
This table shows average, median, maximum, and minimum implied expected recovery rates for the entire firm, senior secured loans, senior unsecured bonds, and senior subordinated bonds as well as average standard deviations of respective recovery rates. Estimates of implied expected recovery rates are obtained using Eqs. (3.14) and (5.6) – (5.8). Estimates of the standard deviation of implied recovery rates are obtained using Eqs. (3.15) and (C.i) – (C.iii). The estimation approach is specified by Eqs. (5.16) and (5.17).

5.4.3 Risk Aversion in Implied Recovery Rates

It was noted earlier that implied expected recovery rates are lower than physical realizations due to the systematic component in recovery risk. Just whether the extent of observed gaps is reasonable, however, is not judged easily. It is the objective of this section to further validate model estimates by calculating the implied degree of investors' aversion to recovery risk. If estimates of implied expected recovery rates are economically meaningful, one would expect risk aversion to be similar for different types of debt and relatively stable over time.

In the following, the work of Bakshi, Madan, and Zhang (2006) is employed. They show that the implied expected recovery rate is related to the probability density of recovery under the physical measure, denoted by ${h_t}^P(x)$, by:

$$E_t^{\tilde{Q}}\left[\rho|1_{\{\tau\leq T\}}=1\right]=\int_0^1\frac{x\,U'(w_0-(1-x)F){h_t}^P(x)}{\int_0^1 U'(w_0-(1-x)F){h_t}^P(x)\,dx}dx \quad (5.18)$$

where $U'(\cdot)=\partial U(\cdot)/\partial x$, $U(\cdot)$ is the utility-of-wealth-function of the representative agent, w_0 is initial wealth, and F is the notional principal at stake (note that the probability of default is not of relevance). From Eq. (5.18) it follows that in the absence of risk aversion, i.e. constant $U'(\cdot)$, expected recovery rates are identical under the T-forward and the physical measure, such that $E_t^{\tilde{Q}}[\rho|1_{\{\tau\le T\}}=1] = E_t^P[\rho]$.[77] However, for concave utility functions, Bakshi et al. show that $\partial E_t^{\tilde{Q}}[\rho|1_{\{\tau\le T\}}=1]/\partial\eta_t < 0$ where η_t is the coefficient of risk aversion. It follows that if $\eta_t > 0$, then $E_t^{\tilde{Q}}[\rho|1_{\{\tau\le T\}}=1] < E_t^P[\rho]$. This relation is intuitive: If investors are risk averse, they require a premium for taking recovery risk which results in implied expected recovery rates being lower than physical expected recovery rates. It was shown earlier that this holds true for the estimates produced by the model.

In the following, it is assumed that the representative agent has an exponential utility function of the form $U(w_t) = -exp(-\eta_t\, w_t)$ where w_t denotes wealth. Exponential utility functions are appealing in that they imply constant risk aversion in absolute dollar terms, irrespective of initial wealth. Therefore, it holds that $-(\partial^2 U(w_t)/\partial {w_t}^2)/(\partial U(w_t)/\partial w_t) = \eta_t$, independently of w_0.[78] Assuming further that $F = 100\%$ and that recovery rates follow a beta distribution, Eq. (5.18) simplifies to:

$$E_t^{\tilde{Q}}[\rho|1_{\{\tau\le T\}}=1] = \frac{C\left(\frac{(1-\mu_t)({\mu_t}^2+{\sigma_t}^2)}{{\sigma_t}^2}, \frac{(1-\mu_t)\mu_t}{{\sigma_t}^2}, -\eta_t\right)\mu_t}{C\left(\frac{((1-\mu_t)\mu_t-{\sigma_t}^2)\mu_t}{{\sigma_t}^2}, \frac{(1-\mu_t)\mu_t}{{\sigma_t}^2}-1, -\eta_t\right)} \tag{5.19}$$

where $C(\cdot)$ is the confluent hypergeometric function and μ_t and σ_t are the mean and standard deviation of the distribution of recovery rates under the physical measure. For a given implied expected recovery rate and the physical distribution of recovery, the resulting η_t can thus be determined.

The physical distribution of recovery at a particular point in time is proxied by the mean and standard deviation of actual recovery rates during the time period starting six months before and ending six months ahead. A narrower interval is found to result in very erratic figures, in particular for senior secured loans and senior subordinated bonds for which observations occur less frequently. Using forward-looking data seems to be justified since the market shows a tendency to anticipate changes in the economic environment by several months.

Figure 5.11 illustrates the evolution of the thusly calculated mean and standard deviation of physical recovery rates between July 2005 and July 2008. Also shown is the evolution of implied expected recovery rates during that time and the resulting coefficient of risk aversion. It is observable that physical recovery rates are at all times higher than implied recovery rates.

---

[77] For constant $U'(\cdot)$, Eq. (5.18) simplifies to $E_t^{\tilde{Q}}[\rho|1_{\{\tau\le T\}}=1] = \int_0^1 \frac{x\, {h_t}^P(x)}{\int_0^1 {h_t}^P(x)dx}dx = E_t^P[\rho]$.

[78] Iso-elastic utility functions, on the other hand, imply that risk aversion is constant in relative terms, i.e. with respect to a particular share of the representative agent's initial wealth.

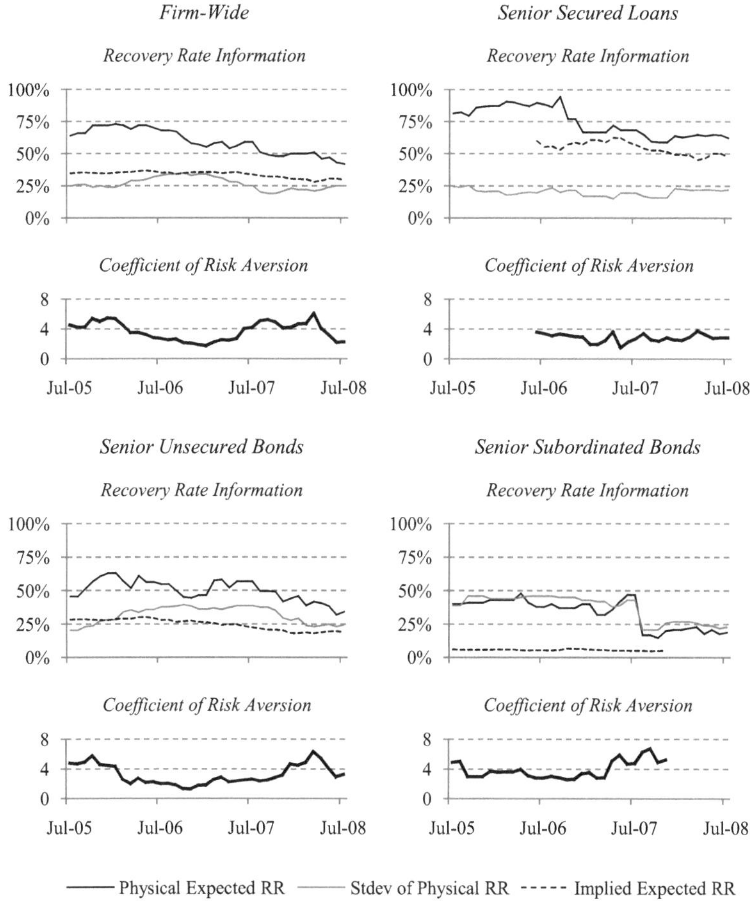

Figure 5.11: Risk Aversion in Implied Expected Recovery Rates
This figure illustrates the evolution of the expected physical recovery rate and its standard deviation. For a particular point in time, these are calculated using actual recovery rates during the time period starting six months before and ending six months ahead. Recovery rates are trading prices 30 days after default of U.S. corporate issuers as reported by Moody's (Hamilton and Varma (2006), Hamilton (2007), Emery, Ou, and Tennant (2008), and Emery and Ou (2009)). The figure also shows the evolution of implied expected recovery rates (averages over all firms) and resulting coefficients of risk aversion. Results are obtained using Eq. (5.19).

For firm-wide recovery rates, η_t fluctuates between 2 and 6, with few exceptions. The average η_t over the entire observation period is 3.7. For recovery rates of senior secured loans, senior unsecured bonds, and senior subordinated bonds, η_t is mostly confined to values between 2 and 6, too, the averages being 2.6, 3.2, and 3.9, respectively. This suggests that the degree of aversion to recovery risk is quite similar for different types of debt but that investors are slightly more risk averse for lower-ranking debt instruments.

A further point to mention is that the tremendous difference between historical and implied expected recovery rates of senior subordinated bonds observed earlier seems to be justified indeed. For example, throughout 2005, the physical expected recovery rate is above 40% while its implied counterpart is slightly below 6%, yet η_t does not exceed 5. This is due to the extraordinarily high standard deviation of the physical expected recovery rate which reaches values up to 46% during that time. This indicates that estimates of implied recovery rates are economically sensible, both, on a firm-wide and on an instrument-specific level.

5.5 Application: Deducing the Implied Probability of Default

The approach to estimating implied recovery rates of Section 5.3 did not require a specification of the link to implied default rates and, in particular, did not presume independence between the two. In Section 5.5.1, estimates of implied expected recovery rates can thus be used to deduce implied probabilities of default without risking that a possible misspecification of this link contaminates results. Section 5.5.2 then examines the relation of both factors under the pricing measure. Finally, in Section 5.5.3, implied probabilities of default are related to physical default rates such that the degree of investors' aversion to default risk can be assessed, similarly as it was done for recovery risk in the previous section.

5.5.1 A Simplistic Approach

To the end of deducing implied probabilities of default, the reduced-form framework developed by Jarrow and Turnbull (1995), Lando (1998), and Duffie and Singleton (1999) is employed once again, such that the probability of default is given by Eq. (2.4). From Eq. (3.6), it then follows that the value of the CDS protection leg under the T-forward measure at time t is given by:

$$PR_t(\rho, T) = \left(1 - E_t^{\tilde{Q}}\left[\rho \mid 1_{\{\tau \leq T\}} = 1\right]\right) E_t^{\tilde{Q}}\left[1 - exp\left(-\int_t^T \lambda_s \, ds\right)\right] B_t(T). \tag{5.20}$$

For ease of expedition, it is supposed that the CDS premium is paid continuously. The value of the annuity at time t is then given by:

$$A_t(T) = E_t^{\tilde{Q}}\left[\int_t^T \frac{1_{\{\tau>s\}}}{B_s(T)} ds\right] B_t(T). \tag{5.21}$$

Setting λ_t equal to the constant default arrival rate $\lambda^{\tilde{Q}}$ and assuming constant interest rates allows expressing Eq. (5.20) as:

$$PR_t(\rho,T) = \left(1 - E_t^{\tilde{Q}}\left[\rho | 1_{\{\tau\leq T\}} = 1\right]\right)\left(1 - exp\left(-\lambda^{\tilde{Q}}(T-t)\right)\right) B_t(T) \tag{5.22}$$

and Eq. (5.21) as:

$$A_t(T) = \frac{\left(exp(r(T-t)) - exp\left(-\lambda^{\tilde{Q}}(T-t)\right)\right) B_t(T)}{\lambda^{\tilde{Q}} + r}. \tag{5.23}$$

Substituting Eqs. (5.22) and (5.23) into Eq. (3.7) and simplifying shows that the CDS premium is then given by:

$$s = \frac{PR_t(\rho,T)}{A_t(T)} = \frac{\left(1 - E_t^{\tilde{Q}}\left[\rho | 1_{\{\tau\leq T\}} = 1\right]\right)\left(\lambda^{\tilde{Q}} + r\right)\left(exp\left(\lambda^{\tilde{Q}}(T-t)\right) - 1\right) B_t(T)}{\left(exp\left(\left(\lambda^{\tilde{Q}} + r\right)(T-t)\right) - 1\right) B_t(T)}. \tag{5.24}$$

Using the first-order approximation $exp(z) \approx 1 + z$, this simplifies to:

$$\begin{aligned} s &\approx \frac{\left(1 - E_t^{\tilde{Q}}\left[\rho | 1_{\{\tau\leq T\}} = 1\right]\right)\lambda^{\tilde{Q}}\left(\lambda^{\tilde{Q}} + r\right)(T-t)B_t(T)}{\left(\lambda^{\tilde{Q}} + r\right)(T-t)B_t(T)} \\ &= \left(1 - E_t^{\tilde{Q}}\left[\rho | 1_{\{\tau\leq T\}} = 1\right]\right)\lambda^{\tilde{Q}}. \end{aligned} \tag{5.25}$$

It then follows that the one-year probability of default under the T-forward measure, denoted by $PD^{\tilde{Q}}$, is approximately given by:

$$PD^{\tilde{Q}} \approx 1 - exp\left(-\frac{s}{1 - E_t^{\tilde{Q}}\left[\rho | 1_{\{\tau\leq T\}} = 1\right]}\right), \tag{5.26}$$

and observed premia and implied expected instrument-specific recovery rates can be used to infer the implied probability of default for a particular firm and at a particular point in time.[79]

Appendix F lists results for each firm, averaged over the respective observation period, and Table 5.9 further aggregates figures over all sample constituents. The average one-year implied probability of default is 2.5% for Sample 1 and 6.3% for Sample 2. The reason for this considerable difference is that Sample 1 firms carry better ratings than Sample 2 firms and that most observations for the latter lie after the outbreak of the sub-prime crisis. Maximum and minimum results vary notably as well, the driver being the divergent credit quality of firms and different observation periods.

	Sample 1	Sample 2
Average	2.5%	6.3%
Median	2.4%	5.6%
Max.	9.1%	14.5%
Min.	0.4%	2.0%
Standard Deviation	1.0%	2.3%

Table 5.9: Implied One-Year Probabilities of Default by Sample
This table shows key statistics of one-year implied probabilities of default for Sample 1 and Sample 2 constituents. Figures are obtained using Eq. (5.26).

	Baa3	Ba1	Ba2	Ba3	B1	B2	B3
Implied	1.0%	2.4%	2.6%	4.8%	6.2%	6.6%	8.6%
Count	2	1	10	6	6	5	4
Historical (Moody's)	0.3%	0.7%	0.7%	1.8%	2.5%	3.8%	7.7%

Table 5.10: Historical vs. Implied One-Year Probabilities of Default
This table shows average implied one-year probabilities of default for firms with the same corporate family rating. Ratings are as published by Moody's and obtained from Bloomberg. For each firm, the average rating during the observation period is used. Estimates are obtained using Eq. (5.26). "Count" indicates the number of firms/issues with a particular rating. Also shown are respective historical one-year default rates, as reported by Emery and Ou (2009) (data from 1983 to 2008).

Table 5.10 shows average implied and physical probabilities of default for firms with the same Moody's corporate family rating. Again, observations are as expected: Physical probabilities are lower than their implied counterparts for all ratings. This indicates that investors

[79] To calculate implied probabilities of default, senior unsecured CDS premia and implied expected recovery rates of senior unsecured bonds are used. It is found that using the respective junior (Sample 1) or senior (Sample 2) instrument leads to virtually identical results (in the absence of estimation error, both would be identical).

require a compensation for taking default risk, a finding consistent with priors (see Fons (1987), Berndt et al. (2005), Driessen (2005), Saita (2006), and Pan and Singleton (2008)).

5.5.2 The Relation to Implied Expected Recovery Rates

Figure 5.12 illustrates the evolution of the average one-year implied probability of default and, for comparison, once more shows the average implied expected firm-wide recovery rate. Throughout 2001, the probability of default sojourned below 2% but increased swiftly in course of the 2002/2003 calamities to levels beyond 12%. 2004 to 2006 was a period of relative calmness, followed by yet another jump around July 2007 and a subsequent increase to around 10% at the end of the observation period.

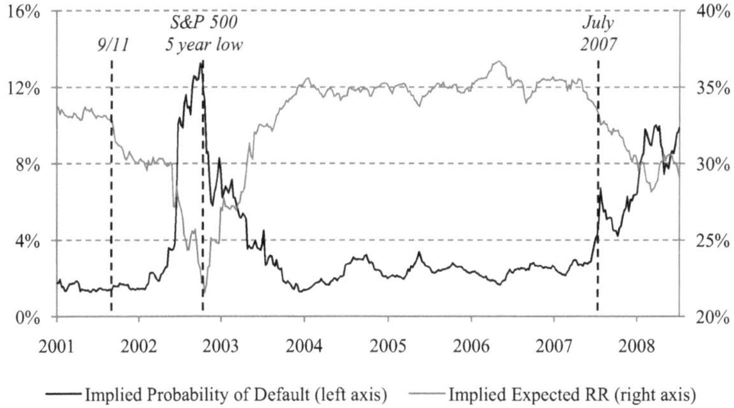

Figure 5.12: Evolution of the Implied Probability of Default
This figure illustrates the evolution of the one-year implied probability of default (obtained using Eq. (5.26) and for comparison once more shows the evolution of the implied expected firm-wide recovery rate. Figures are averages over all firms.

Also, it is observable that the relation to the recovery rate is strongly negative. An ordinary least squares regression suggests that a one percentage point increase in the probability of default is on average associated with a 17.8 BP decrease in the recovery rate, significant at the 1% confidence level. This is in accordance with research cited earlier, showing that default and recovery rates are negatively related, both, under the physical measure (i.e. Cantor and Varma (2005) and Acharya, Bharath, and Srinivasan (2006)) and under the risk-neutral measure (Bakshi, Madan, and Zhang (2006) and Das and Hanouna (2009)).

5.5.3 *Risk Aversion in the Implied Probability of Default*

The objective of this section is analogous to that of Section 5.4.3: The (observable) gap between implied and physical probabilities of default is used to calculate investors' aversion to default risk. Results are then compared to those obtained for recovery risk, such that the reliability of estimates can be assessed further. To that end, the framework of Bakshi, Madan, and Zhang (2006) is employed once again. They show that the implied probability of default is related to the physical probability of default, denoted by PD_t^P, and the physical probability density of recovery by:

$$PD_t^{\tilde{Q}} = \frac{PD_t^P \int_0^1 U'(w_0 - (1-x)F) h_t^P(x)\, dx}{(1 - PD_t^P) U'(w_0) + PD_t^P \int_0^1 U'(w_0 - (1-x)F) h_t^P(x)\, dx}. \tag{5.27}$$

Thus, risk aversion in the probability of default cannot be analyzed independently of recovery risk. To see why this is, consider the hypothetical case of full expected recovery: If $E_t^P[\rho] = 1$, it holds true that $\int_0^1 U'(w_0 - (1-x)F) h_t^P(x)\, dx = U'(w_0)$ which implies that probabilities of default are identical under the T-forward and the physical measure, i.e. $PD_t^{\tilde{Q}} = PD_t^P$. Absence of risk aversion leads to the same result.[80] For $E_t^P[\rho] < 1$ and concave utility functions, however, it holds true that $\int_0^1 U'(w_0 - (1-x)F) h_t^P(x)\, dx > U'(w_0)$ which implies $PD_t^{\tilde{Q}} > PD_t^P$. This relation is intuitive, too: If investors are risk averse, they require a premium for taking default risk which results in the probability of default being higher under the pricing than under the physical measure.

Under the same assumptions as employed in Section 5.4.3, Eq. (5.27) simplifies to:

$$PD_t^{\tilde{Q}} = 1 + \left(\frac{C\left(\frac{(\mu_t - 1)^2 \mu_t}{{\sigma_t}^2} + \mu_t - 1, \frac{(1-\mu_t)\mu_t}{{\sigma_t}^2} - 1, \eta_t \right) PD_t^P}{PD_t^P - 1} - 1 \right)^{-1} \tag{5.28}$$

where, as in Section 5.4.3, $C(\cdot)$ is the confluent hypergeometric function and μ_t and σ_t are the mean and the standard deviation of the distribution of recovery rates under the physical measure. Given (implied and physical) probabilities of default and the physical distribution of recovery rates, the resulting coefficient of risk aversion η_t can thus be determined.

---

[80] For constant $U'(\cdot)$, Eq. (5.27) simplifies to $PD_t^{\tilde{Q}} = \frac{PD_t^P \int_0^1 h_t^P(x)dx}{(1-PD_t^P) + PD_t^P \int_0^1 h_t^P(x)dx} = PD_t^P$.

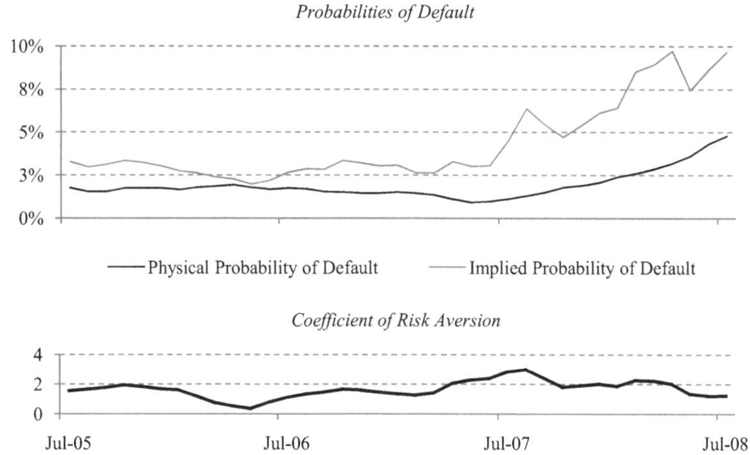

Figure 5.13: Risk Aversion in the Implied Probability of Default
This figure illustrates the evolution of the physical and the implied probability of default. The physical probability for a particular point in time is calculated using actual default rates of sub-investment grade corporate issuers during the time period starting six months before and ending six months ahead. Data are taken from Moody's (Emery and Ou (2009)). The implied probability is obtained by averaging over all firms with a sub-investment grade Moody's corporate family rating. The figure also shows the resulting coefficient of risk aversion for the calculation of which the mean and standard deviation of the distribution of firm-wide recovery rates under the physical measure are used additionally. Results are obtained using Eq. (5.28).

Figure 5.13 illustrates the evolution of one-year physical and implied probabilities of default. The physical probability at a particular point in time is approximated using the average default rate of U.S. sub-investment grade corporate issuers during the time period starting six months before and ending six months ahead. To assure comparability, the implied probability is calculated using only those firms with a sub-investment grade rating. Also shown is the resulting coefficient of risk aversion, for the calculation of which the mean and standard deviation of the physical distribution of firm-wide recovery rates are used additionally. It is observable that the physical probability of default is at all times lower than its implied counterpart and that both start off to new heights around July 2007. η_t fluctuates between 1 and 3, with one exception in the first half of 2006, where both probabilities almost cross. The average η_t over the entire observation period is 1.7 and thus somewhat lower than the η_ts obtained for recovery risk (firm-wide: 3.7). This might be attributable to the fact that default risk is more researched and better understood than recovery risk, making investors more comfortable with taking the first than the second. Further, it was mentioned earlier that in practice, the relative scarcity of default events impedes an efficient diversification even of the idiosyncratic component of recovery risk, possibly a further reason for investors requiring a higher compensation.

6 Conclusion and Outlook

This thesis pursues a new approach to estimating market-implied recovery rates, exploiting the fact that differently-ranking debt instruments of a given issuer face identical arrival risk but different default-conditional recovery rates. It is shown that employing (L)CDSs on two such instruments, it is feasible to construct a metric that is a function only of implied expected recovery rates but void of default risk. Based on this metric and additionally taking into consideration capital structure data, a firm's entire implied probability distribution of recovery at a particular point in time can be inferred. This proceeding stands out perspicuously against those of priors in that the identification problem is overcome without imposing an assumption-heavy model structure. Most importantly, the pricing measure is chosen such that recovery risk can be separated from default risk without presuming independence.

The practical implementation of the approach rests upon a unique and carefully constructed data set: Screening the universe of outstanding CDSs reveals that the overwhelming majority of instruments references either senior unsecured bonds or senior subordinated bonds, and a number of firms is identified for which both exist. Alternative combinations are unworkable as seniorities other than the mentioned are referenced only in negligibly few cases. To broaden the basis of the investigation nonetheless, advantage is taken of LCDSs, a new type of credit derivative that has emerged in recent years. LCDS data has become available for a relatively large number of issuers such that a second data set can be composed, this time containing firms on which LCDSs as well as CDSs on senior unsecured bonds are outstanding.

Results suggest that the implied probability distribution of recovery is related to proxies for firm- and industry-specific financial health. In particular, implied expected recovery rates tend to be higher for issuers with low leverage, a high share of tangible assets, strong liquidity, and more so if an issuer's industry is in a robust condition. This extends earlier findings on the determinants of physical recovery rates such as Cantor and Varma (2005) or Acharya, Bharath, and Srinivasan (2007) to the risk-neutral world.

Of particular interest is the fact that the shape of the implied probability density of recovery differs significantly from that of its physical counterpart: While the physical density is known to be approximately bell-shaped, the implied density is U-shaped due to the high standard deviation of implied recovery rates. This suggests that ex ante there is substantial uncertainty as to where recovery rates will come out in the event of a default, a proposition most practitioners would probably endorse.

Instrument-specific recovery rates are first and foremost driven by the reference obligation's seniority and the issuer's capital structure. Implied expected recovery rates are found to be on average more than twice as high for senior secured loans as for senior unsecured bonds and more than four times as high for senior unsecured bonds as for senior subordinated bonds. Further, within a particular type of debt, significant inter-company differences exist. Quantifying the sensitivity of recovery rates to the size of debt cushion below and above suggests that capital structure characteristics explain most of these differences. In addition, it is examined whether implied expected firm-wide recovery rates are related to corporate family ratings but no evidence is found in this respect. This is consistent with Emery (2007) who does the same for historical recovery rates and likewise detects no such link. The picture is, however, quite different when instrument-specific ratings are considered as these explicitly account for the recovery prospects of a particular debt issue.

The observation period includes two phases of major economic shakeups, namely the time from 2001 to 2003 which was characterized by the repercussions from the burst of the internet bubble and the time from summer 2007 to July 2008 when the sub-prime crisis started to unfold. It is observable that implied expected recovery rates are strongly affected by the economic environment, falling substantially in times of distress and reverting to a "non-crisis-level" in between. This concurs with earlier research such as Altman, Brady, Resti, and Sironi (2005) or Chava, Stefanescu, and Turnbull (2008) which shows that historically, recovery rates were higher when the economy fared well. The standard deviation of implied recovery rates, though, behaves contrarily, generally rising in times of distress. This indicates that there is a systematic component in recovery risk, such that implied expected recovery rates should on average be lower than comparable physical realizations.

To validate results, the model is re-calibrated based on two alternative parameterizations of the implied probability distribution of recovery. Estimation results, however, do not differ materially and, in particular, the U-shape of implied distribution persists. Further, estimates of implied expected recovery rates are related to actual recovery rates, revealing that the first are significantly lower than the second, thus confirming that investors indeed require a premium for taking recovery risk. Using an exponential utility function, the coefficients of risk aversion for firm-wide and instrument-specific recovery rates are calculated with results suggesting that investors are somewhat more risk averse for lower-ranking debt instruments.

Finally, estimates of implied expected recovery rates are used to deduce implied probabilities of default. This is feasible since the approach to estimating recovery rates did not impose any relationship upon default and recovery rates. Implied probabilities of default exhibit a strong dependency on the economic environment, too, rising substantially in times of distress. Consequently, they are inversely related to implied expected recovery rates, a result consistent with Bakshi, Madan, and Zhang (2006) and Das and Hanouna (2009). Further, the coefficient of risk aversion for the implied probability of default is found to be lower than that for implied recovery rates, possibly due to investors being more comfortable with taking default risk than with taking (the less understood) recovery risk.

These results enhance our understanding of implied recovery considerably and should be of interest to practitioners and researchers alike. Traders, for instance, should know that the market practice of pricing senior unsecured CDSs with an implied recovery rate of 40%, while being in accordance with historical observations, does not take into consideration the current economic prospects nor does it entail a compensation for the systematic factor in recovery risk. The market rather sees this figure at around 25% and even lower in times of (expected) financial distress.

Further, a separate identification of implied default and recovery rates is indispensable for the pricing of derivatives that are a function only of either factor. Marking-to-market premium legs of seasoned CDSs, for instance, requires as input the implied probability of default and not the total expected loss. The same is true for the pricing of digital default swaps. Recovery swaps, on the other hand, are a function only of the implied expected recovery rate and a precise estimate of this figure is needed to assure arbitrage-free relationships to other instruments.

There is abundant literature indicating that factors other than expected loss, such as liquidity and counterparty risk, are of relevance for the pricing of CDSs, as well, and more so for higher ratings (see Janosi, Jarrow, and Yildirim (2002), Longstaff, Mithal, and Neis (2005), Ericsson and Renault (2006), and others). For the sake of simplicity, these where disregarded in this thesis, and the fact that most sample firms have a sub-investment grade rating probably extenuates the issue. An extension of the model in this direction would be of interest nonetheless, in particular in light of the recent events.

Appendices

A Supremum and Infimum Standard Deviations

A.I Beta Distribution

The mean and the variance of the beta distribution are:

$$\mu = \int_0^1 x bet(x) dx = \frac{p}{p+q}, \tag{A.I.i}$$

$$\sigma^2 = \int_0^1 (x-\mu)^2 bet(x) dx = \frac{pq}{(p+q)^2(p+q+1)} \quad p, q \in]0, \infty[. \tag{A.I.ii}$$

Solving Eq. ((A.I.i) for q and substituting into Eq. ((A.I.ii) gives:

$$\begin{aligned} \sigma &= \sqrt{\frac{p\frac{(1-\mu)p}{\mu}}{\left(p+\frac{(1-\mu)p}{\mu}\right)^2\left(p+\frac{(1-\mu)p}{\mu}+1\right)}} \\ &= \sqrt{\frac{(1-\mu)}{\left(1+\frac{(1-\mu)}{\mu}\right)^2\left(p+\frac{(1-\mu)p}{\mu}+1\right)\mu}} \\ &= \sqrt{\frac{(1-\mu)}{\left(\frac{\mu+p}{\mu^3}\right)\mu}} = \sqrt{\frac{(1-\mu)\mu^2}{\mu+p}}. \end{aligned} \tag{A.I.iii}$$

Subject to the constraint $p > 0$, the supremum and infimum of the standard deviation for a given μ thus are:

$$\sigma_{sup} = \lim_{p \to 0} \sqrt{\frac{(1-\mu)\mu^2}{\mu + p}} = \sqrt{\mu - \mu^2} \quad \mu \in]0,1[, \tag{A.I.iv}$$

$$\sigma_{inf} = \lim_{p \to \infty} \sqrt{\frac{(1-\mu)\mu^2}{\mu + p}} = 0. \tag{A.I.v}$$

A.II Transformed Normal Distribution

Güntay, Madan, and Unal (2003) show that the mean and variance of the transformed normal distribution are:

$$\mu = 1 - \int_0^1 N\left(\frac{log\left(\frac{x}{1-x}\right) - \bar{\mu}}{\bar{\sigma}}\right) dx, \tag{A.II.i}$$

$$\sigma^2 = 2\int_0^1 (1-x) N\left(\frac{log\left(\frac{x}{1-x}\right) - \bar{\mu}}{\bar{\sigma}}\right) dx - \left(\int_0^1 N\left(\frac{log\left(\frac{x}{1-x}\right) - \bar{\mu}}{\bar{\sigma}}\right) dx\right)^2 \tag{A.II.ii}$$

where $N(\cdot)$ is the cumulative normal distribution function.

From Eqs. (A.II.i) and (A.II.ii) it follows that the variance can be expressed as a function of μ and a residual term:

$$\sigma^2 = \mu - \mu^2 - 2\int_0^1 \left(x - \frac{1}{2}\right) N\left(\frac{log\left(\frac{x}{1-x}\right) - \bar{\mu}}{\bar{\sigma}}\right) dx. \tag{A.II.iii}$$

Since $N\left(\frac{log\left(\frac{x}{1-x}\right)-\bar{\mu}}{\bar{\sigma}}\right)$ is monotonously increasing in x, $\int_0^1 \left(x - \frac{1}{2}\right) N\left(\frac{log\left(\frac{x}{1-x}\right)-\bar{\mu}}{\bar{\sigma}}\right) dx$ is positive.

Hence, $\sigma_{sup} = \sqrt{\mu - \mu^2}$ is equivalent to:

$$\inf_{(\bar{\mu},\bar{\sigma})} \int_0^1 \left(x - \frac{1}{2}\right) N\left(\frac{log\left(\frac{x}{1-x}\right) - \bar{\mu}}{\bar{\sigma}}\right) dx = 0 \qquad (A.II.iv)$$

$$s.t.\, 1 - \int_0^1 N\left(\frac{log\left(\frac{x}{1-x}\right) - \bar{\mu}}{\bar{\sigma}}\right) dx = \mu.$$

For all $\bar{\sigma} \in]0, \infty[$ one can find a $\bar{\mu}$ satisfying $1 - \int_0^1 N\left(\frac{log\left(\frac{x}{1-x}\right) - \bar{\mu}}{\bar{\sigma}}\right) dx = \mu$ where μ is arbitrary but fixed in $]0,1[$. This allows constructing a sequence $(\bar{\mu}_n, \bar{\sigma}_n)$ such that $\bar{\sigma}_n \to \infty$ and $1 - \int_0^1 N\left(\frac{log\left(\frac{x}{1-x}\right) - \bar{\mu}_n}{\bar{\sigma}_n}\right) dx = \mu.$

Next, it is shown that:

$$\lim_{n\to\infty} \int_0^1 \left(x - \frac{1}{2}\right) N\left(\frac{log\left(\frac{x}{1-x}\right) - \bar{\mu}_n}{\bar{\sigma}_n}\right) dx = 0 \qquad (A.II.v)$$

$$s.t.\, 1 - \int_0^1 N\left(\frac{log\left(\frac{x}{1-x}\right) - \bar{\mu}_n}{\bar{\sigma}_n}\right) dx = \mu.$$

Note that for all $\tilde{\varepsilon}$, the difference $N\left(\frac{log\left(\frac{x}{1-x}\right) - \bar{\mu}_n}{\bar{\sigma}_n}\right) - N\left(-\frac{\bar{\mu}_n}{\bar{\sigma}_n}\right)$ converges to zero uniformly in $[\tilde{\varepsilon}, 1 - \tilde{\varepsilon}]$. Therefore, for all $\varepsilon > 0$ and setting $\tilde{\varepsilon} = 1/2\varepsilon$, there exists an n^* such that:

$$N\left(\frac{log\left(\frac{x}{1-x}\right) - \bar{\mu}_{n^*}}{\bar{\sigma}_{n^*}}\right) - N\left(-\frac{\bar{\mu}_{n^*}}{\bar{\sigma}_{n^*}}\right) < \varepsilon \quad x \in [\tilde{\varepsilon}, 1 - \tilde{\varepsilon}]. \qquad (A.II.vi)$$

Thus:

$$\int_0^1 \left(x-\frac{1}{2}\right) N\left(\frac{log\left(\frac{x}{1-x}\right)-\bar{\mu}_n}{\bar{\sigma}_n}\right) dx \qquad (A.II.vii)$$

$$= \int_0^1 \left(x-\frac{1}{2}\right)\left(N\left(\frac{log\left(\frac{x}{1-x}\right)-\bar{\mu}_{n^*}}{\bar{\sigma}_{n^*}}\right) - N\left(-\frac{\bar{\mu}_{n^*}}{\bar{\sigma}_{n^*}}\right)\right) dx$$

$$= \int_0^{\tilde{\varepsilon}} \left(x-\frac{1}{2}\right)\left(N\left(\frac{log\left(\frac{x}{1-x}\right)-\bar{\mu}_{n^*}}{\bar{\sigma}_{n^*}}\right) - N\left(-\frac{\bar{\mu}_{n^*}}{\bar{\sigma}_{n^*}}\right)\right) dx$$

$$+ \int_{\tilde{\varepsilon}}^{1-\tilde{\varepsilon}} \left(x-\frac{1}{2}\right)\left(N\left(\frac{log\left(\frac{x}{1-x}\right)-\bar{\mu}_{n^*}}{\bar{\sigma}_{n^*}}\right) - N\left(-\frac{\bar{\mu}_{n^*}}{\bar{\sigma}_{n^*}}\right)\right) dx$$

$$+ \int_{1-\tilde{\varepsilon}}^{1} \left(x-\frac{1}{2}\right)\left(N\left(\frac{log\left(\frac{x}{1-x}\right)-\bar{\mu}_{n^*}}{\bar{\sigma}_{n^*}}\right) - N\left(-\frac{\bar{\mu}_{n^*}}{\bar{\sigma}_{n^*}}\right)\right) dx$$

$$< \varepsilon \,.$$

This satisfies Eq. (A.II.iv). The supremum of the standard deviation of the transformed normal distribution for a given μ thus is:

$$\sigma_{sup} = \sqrt{\mu - \mu^2} \quad \mu \in \,]0{,}1[. \qquad (A.II.viii)$$

In an analogous argument, it can be shown that there is a sequence $(\bar{\mu}_n, \bar{\sigma}_n)$ such that $\bar{\sigma}_n \to 0$ and $1 - \int_0^1 N\left(\frac{log\left(\frac{x}{1-x}\right)-\bar{\mu}_n}{\bar{\sigma}_n}\right) dx = \mu$.

The infimum of the standard deviation of the transformed normal distribution for a given μ thus is:

$$\sigma_{inf} = 0. \qquad (A.II.ix)$$

A.III Quadratic Distribution

From $\int_0^1 u(x)\, dx = 1$ it follows that:

$$a_0 = 1 - \frac{a_2}{12}. \tag{A.III.i}$$

Substituting Eq. (A.III.i) into the density function of the quadratic distribution shows that the mean of the quadratic distribution is given by:

$$\mu = \int_0^1 x\, u(x)\, dx = \frac{1}{2} + \frac{a_1}{12} \tag{A.III.ii}$$

and that the variance of the quadratic distribution is given by:

$$\sigma^2 = \int_0^1 (x - \mu)^2\, u(x)\, dx = \frac{1}{12} - \frac{{a_1}^2}{144} + \frac{a_2}{180}. \tag{A.III.iii}$$

To satisfy $u(x) \geq 0$ for all $x \in [0,1]$, it is required that $u(0) \geq 0$ and $u(1) \geq 0$ if the function is concave and $u(x') \geq 0$ where $\partial u(x')/\partial x = 0$ if the function is convex. This results in side conditions $a_0 - 1/2a_1 + 1/4a_2 \geq 0$, $a_0 + 1/2a_1 + 1/4a_2 \geq 0$, and $a_0 - {a_1}^2/4a_2 \geq 0$.

Substituting Eq. (A.III.i) and (A.III.ii) into Eq. (A.III.iii) shows that the maximization/minimization problem is given by:

$$\underset{a_2}{max/min} \sqrt{\frac{1}{12} - \frac{(12\mu - 6)^2}{144} + \frac{a_2}{180}} \tag{A.III.iv}$$

$$s.t.\ \ 6\mu - 3 - \frac{a_2}{4} \geq 0, 3 - 6\mu - \frac{a_2}{4} \geq 0, 1 - \frac{a_2}{12} - \frac{(12\mu - 6)^2}{4a_2} \geq 0.$$

Applying standard optimization techniques yields the maximum and minimum standard deviation of the quadratic distribution for a given μ:

$$\sigma_{max} = \sqrt{\mu - \mu^2 + \frac{\sqrt{3\mu(1-\mu) - \frac{1}{2}} - 2}{15}} \qquad \mu \in \left[\frac{1}{2} - \frac{\sqrt{3}}{6}, \frac{1}{2} + \frac{\sqrt{3}}{6}\right], \tag{A.III.v}$$

$$\sigma_{min} = \begin{cases} \sqrt{\mu - \mu^2 - \dfrac{\sqrt{3\mu(1-\mu) - \frac{1}{2}} + 2}{15}} & \mu \in \left[\dfrac{1}{2} - \dfrac{\sqrt{3}}{6}, \dfrac{1}{4}\right] \cup \left]\dfrac{3}{4}, \dfrac{1}{2} + \dfrac{\sqrt{3}}{6}\right] \\ \sqrt{\dfrac{4}{5}\mu - \mu^2 - \dfrac{1}{10}} & \mu \in \left]\dfrac{1}{4}, \dfrac{1}{2}\right] \\ \sqrt{\dfrac{6}{5}\mu - \mu^2 - \dfrac{3}{10}} & \mu \in \left]\dfrac{1}{2}, \dfrac{3}{4}\right] \end{cases} \quad . \tag{A.III.vi}$$

B Descriptive Statistics by Firm

Sample 1 Constituents

	Amkor Technology Inc.	Best Buy Co. Inc.	Boyd Gaming Corp.	Cox Communications Inc.	D.R. Horton Inc.	Harrah's Entertainment Inc.	Health Management Associates Inc.	KB Home	MGM Mirage	Solectron Corp.
Ticker Symbol	AMKR	BBY*	BYD	COX*	DHI	HET*	HMA*	KBH	MGM	SLR
SIC Code	367	573	799	484	153	799	806	153	799	367
Observations (Weekly)										
First	Jun-02	May-03	Oct-04	Jan-01	Mar-06	Dec-04	Sep-06	Apr-04	Jun-04	Apr-06
Last	Dec-07	Dec-07	Dec-07	Dec-05	Sep-07	Dec-07	Dec-07	Nov-07	Dec-07	Aug-06
Count	286	241	166	261	81	154	63	189	183	21
Moody's Corporate Family Rating	B1, B2	Baa3	Ba2	NA	Ba2	B3	Ba3	Ba1	Ba1, Ba2	B1
Senior Unsecured CDS Premia (BPs)										
Average	626	44	200	119	132	157	199	178	181	187
Median	542	39	183	95	97	75	135	151	171	187
Max.	1,777	129	485	500	411	609	411	517	514	215
Min.	214	24	108	35	56	47	89	66	113	149
Senior Subordinated CDS Premia (BPs)										
Average	863	70	214	206	165	185	231	228	230	276
Median	800	59	197	163	132	81	166	197	222	255
Max.	2,179	296	473	852	458	671	445	583	538	332
Min.	326	31	140	40	76	51	121	96	163	210
Avg. Ratio	73.5%	68.9%	92.5%	69.8%	76.9%	85.9%	83.3%	77.2%	78.2%	68.4%
Avg. Diff. (BPs)	237	27	15	87	32	28	32	50	49	88

Sample 1 Constituents (Cont'd)

	Station Casinos Inc.	TJX Cos. Inc.	Toll Brothers Inc.	Triad Hospitals Inc.	TRW Automotive Inc.	Tesoro Corp.	United Rentals Inc.	Average
Ticker Symbol	STN	TJX*	TOL*	TRI	TRW	TSO*	URI	
SIC Code	799	565	153	806	371	131	735	
Observations (Weekly)								
First	Sep-04	3-16-3	Mar-04	Jul-04	Jan-05	Nov-04	Jul-04	
Last	Dec-07	Dec-07	Oct-07	Dec-06	Dec-07	Sep-06	Dec-07	
Count	170	219	188	129	151	95	180	163
Moody's Corporate Family Rating	Ba2, B2	NA	Baa3	NA	Ba2	Ba3, Ba1	B2	
Senior Unsecured CDS Premia (BPs)								
Average	180	27	93	181	219	100	286	183
Median	157	26	81	163	208	95	258	
Max.	501	56	297	278	420	158	744	
Min.	95	14	45	134	127	78	150	
Senior Subordinated CDS Premia (BPs)								
Average	233	41	122	253	262	151	397	243
Median	203	45	110	242	258	151	371	
Max.	634	65	330	361	465	259	814	
Min.	141	17	63	188	181	99	260	
Avg. Ratio	76.3%	68.4%	75.5%	71.5%	83.1%	69.4%	70.4%	75.8%
Avg. Diff. (BPs)	53	15	28	72	42	51	111	60

Sample 2 Constituents

	Advanced Micro Devices Inc.	ArvinMeritor Inc.	Allied Waste North America Inc.	Cablevision Systems Corp.	Dean Foods Co.	Directv Holdings LLC.	El Paso Corp.	Ford Motor Co.	Freeport McMoran Copper & Gold Inc.	Freescale Semiconductor Inc.
Ticker Symbol	AMD	ARM*	AW	CVC	DF*	DTV	EP	F*	FCX	FSL
SIC Code	367	371	495	484	202	484	492	371	102	367
Observations										
First	Mar-07	Sep-07	Feb-07	Jun-06	Apr-07	Dec-06	May-06	Dec-06	Mar-07	Mar-07
Last	Aug-07	Jun-08	Jul-08	Jul-08	Jul-08	Jul-08	Jul-08	Jul-08	Sep-07	Jul-08
Count	24	40	74	110	67	81	114	81	29	71
Moody's Corporate Family Rating	B1	Ba3, B1	NA	NA	Ba3, B1	Ba2	B3, Ba3	B3	Ba2	Ba3, B1
LCDS Premia (BPs)										
Average	181	350	193	192	245	139	126	421	62	334
Median	137	340	160	144	260	150	120	415	60	350
Max.	380	495	370	445	450	270	275	915	90	650
Min.	100	200	85	75	75	52	45	169	50	94
Senior Unsecured CDS Premia (BPs)										
Average	438	642	320	309	334	224	181	731	104	674
Median	383	650	328	264	345	196	181	674	98	632
Max.	710	868	499	575	606	370	335	1,643	181	1,231
Min.	293	320	158	148	122	121	91	419	87	290
Avg. Ratio	40.0%	55.0%	58.0%	60.3%	72.7%	61.2%	66.7%	55.2%	60.6%	48.0%
Avg. Diff. (BPs)	257	292	127	117	89	85	55	310	42	340

Sample 2 Constituents (Cont'd)

	Hospital Corporation of America Inc.	Idearc Inc.	Lear Corp.	Michaels Stores Inc.	Realogy Corp.	Sungard Data Systems Inc.	Tribune Co.	TRW Automotive Inc.	Univision Communications Inc.	Visteon Corp.	Average
Ticker Symbol	HCA*	IDARQ*	LEA*	MIKE	REAL*	SGDS	TRB*	TRW	UVN*	VSTN*	
SIC Code	806	274	371	594	653	737	271	371	483	371	
Observations											
First	Nov-06	Jul-07	Jun-07	Jun-07	May-07	Aug-07	May-07	Mar-07	Mar-07	Sep-06	
Last	Jul-08	Jul-08	Jul-08	Jan-08	Jul-08	Jul-08	Nov-07	Jul-08	Jul-08	Jul-08	
Count	88	54	56	33	61	50	25	69	69	95	65
Moody's Corporate Family Rating	Ba2	Ba3, B1	B2	B2	B3	B2	Ba3	Ba2	B1	B2, B3	
LCDS Premia (BPs)											
Average	226	407	324	299	854	290	411	181	457	478	309
Median	248	295	300	300	615	275	460	175	375	375	
Max.	435	800	560	480	2,017	505	545	360	885	1,372	
Min.	80	140	200	130	240	150	215	80	145	140	
Senior Unsecured CDS Premia (BPs)											
Average	384	654	522	465	1,523	442	726	339	838	865	536
Median	388	436	482	447	1,625	431	834	329	587	739	
Max.	599	1,556	851	724	2,716	620	902	632	2,148	2,136	
Min.	241	190	310	273	477	293	419	174	335	373	
Avg. Ratio	56.1%	68.4%	61.9%	63.4%	54.8%	64.7%	56.2%	52.9%	55.3%	51.1%	58.1%
Avg. Diff. (BPs)	159	247	198	166	668	152	315	159	380	387	227

For each of the firms in Sample 1 and Sample 2, this table shows, where applicable, ticker symbols, three digit SIC codes, observation periods, the number of (weekly) observations, the first and last Moody's corporate family rating in the respective observation period, LCDS premia, senior unsecured CDS premia, senior subordinated CDS premia, ratios of premia (defined as s_{uns}/s_{sub} for Sample 1 constituents and as s_{loan}/s_{uns} for Sample 2 constituents), and differences of premia (defined as $s_{sub} - s_{uns}$ for Sample 1 constituents and as $s_{uns} - s_{loan}$ for Sample 2 constituents). * indicates that CDS terms of the respective firm stipulate MR as a credit event (XR otherwise). Premia of respective CDSs are adjusted to XR by multiplying with 0.9465.

C The Variance of Implied Expected Recovery Rates

For a given probability density function of recovery given default $h_t(x)$, the variances of implied expected recovery rates of senior secured loans, senior unsecured bonds, and senior subordinated bonds are given by:

$$Var_t^{\tilde{Q}}[\rho_{loan} \,|1_{\{\tau\leq T\}} = 1] = \int_0^a \left(\frac{x}{loan} - E_t^{\tilde{Q}}[\rho_{loan} \,|1_{\{\tau\leq T\}} = 1]\right)^2 h_t(x)dx + \int_a^1 \left(1 - E_t^{\tilde{Q}}[\rho_{loan} \,|1_{\{\tau\leq T\}} = 1]\right)^2 h_t(x)dx, \quad (C.i)$$

$$Var_t^{\tilde{Q}}[\rho_{uns} \,|1_{\{\tau\leq T\}} = 1] = \int_b^c \left(\frac{x-b}{uns} - E_t^{\tilde{Q}}[\rho_{uns} \,|1_{\{\tau\leq T\}} = 1]\right)^2 h_t(x)dx + \int_c^1 \left(1 - E_t^{\tilde{Q}}[\rho_{uns} \,|1_{\{\tau\leq T\}} = 1]\right)^2 h_t(x)dx, \quad (C.ii)$$

$$Var_t^{\tilde{Q}}[\rho_{sub} \,|1_{\{\tau\leq T\}} = 1] = \int_c^1 \left(\frac{x-c}{sub} - E_t^{\tilde{Q}}[\rho_{sub} \,|1_{\{\tau\leq T\}} = 1]\right)^2 h_t(x)dx\,. \quad (C.iii)$$

D Implied Recovery Rates by Firm

Sample 1 Constituents

	AMKR	BBY	BYD	COX	DHI	HET	HMA	KBH	MGM	SLR
Firm-Wide Recovery Rate										
Implied Expected	34.4%	36.2%	33.4%	30.5%	33.4%	33.2%	38.8%	35.1%	32.5%	41.0%
Stdev.	32.8%	32.8%	32.0%	32.0%	31.8%	31.9%	33.3%	32.4%	31.8%	32.8%
Recovery Rate of Senior Unsecured Bonds										
Implied Expected	36.0%	36.9%	22.7%	22.4%	22.5%	22.8%	22.6%	26.4%	21.5%	42.9%
Stdev.	39.8%	34.2%	39.4%	34.1%	32.7%	34.7%	39.1%	37.7%	35.3%	34.2%
Recovery Rate of Senior Subordintd Bonds										
Implied Expected	9.3%	2.7%	9.4%	3.1%	1.4%	3.8%	10.0%	6.3%	4.7%	3.6%
Stdev.	24.3%	13.7%	23.9%	12.1%	9.8%	15.9%	24.9%	20.2%	17.6%	15.7%

	STN	TJX	TOL	TRI	TRW	TSO	URI	Avg.
Firm-Wide Recovery Rate								
Implied Expected	31.8%	34.0%	35.2%	40.0%	34.8%	35.3%	36.1%	35.0%
Stdev.	31.6%	32.2%	32.4%	33.1%	32.3%	32.2%	32.6%	32.3%
Recovery Rate of Senior Unsecured Bonds								
Implied Expected	25.8%	30.7%	33.3%	33.0%	23.3%	28.3%	31.4%	28.4%
Stdev.	39.8%	34.7%	36.9%	41.9%	33.9%	36.3%	41.2%	36.8%
Recovery Rate of Senior Subordintd Bonds								
Implied Expected	8.8%	2.6%	5.2%	11.2%	2.0%	4.1%	10.1%	5.8%
Stdev.	23.3%	13.3%	18.5%	26.3%	11.9%	15.8%	24.9%	18.4%

Sample 2 Constituents

	AMD	ARM	AW	CVC	DF	DTV	EP	F	FCX	FSL
Firm-Wide Recovery Rate										
Implied Expected	37.3%	30.9%	30.3%	29.8%	31.7%	34.6%	30.9%	32.3%	38.5%	36.1%
Stdev.	33.0%	33.4%	32.4%	31.7%	33.0%	33.4%	32.0%	32.8%	33.4%	34.0%
Recovery Rate of Senior Secured Loans										
Implied Expected	75.7%	59.2%	54.1%	47.0%	41.6%	58.9%	51.2%	59.7%	68.9%	68.9%
Stdev.	37.5%	43.5%	43.0%	41.5%	39.6%	42.0%	41.8%	42.3%	39.6%	40.5%
Recovery Rate of Senior Unsecured Bonds										
Implied Expected	31.6%	23.8%	12.3%	16.3%	11.8%	23.3%	17.7%	24.7%	28.7%	40.3%
Stdev.	34.3%	33.6%	27.3%	30.8%	26.9%	33.5%	30.2%	34.5%	34.7%	43.4%

	HCA	IDARQ	LEA	MIKE	REAL	SGDS	TRB	TRW	UVN	VSTN	Avg.
Firm-Wide Recovery Rate											
Implied Expected	33.5%	27.3%	31.4%	22.7%	30.2%	32.6%	31.8%	33.3%	30.7%	32.8%	31.9%
Stdev.	33.0%	31.9%	33.2%	29.2%	32.7%	33.7%	32.3%	33.4%	32.5%	32.8%	32.7%
Recovery Rate of Senior Secured Loans											
Implied Expected	49.3%	36.3%	51.0%	36.7%	49.1%	45.5%	52.8%	54.6%	54.4%	60.0%	53.7%
Stdev.	41.2%	39.1%	42.8%	40.3%	42.4%	41.3%	42.2%	42.5%	43.0%	42.1%	41.4%
Recovery Rate of Senior Unsecured Bonds											
Implied Expected	11.8%	10.0%	19.3%	12.9%	17.1%	18.7%	19.0%	22.4%	20.8%	23.4%	20.3%
Stdev.	26.9%	25.1%	32.0%	29.2%	33.2%	35.2%	31.5%	34.6%	32.1%	32.9%	32.1%

For each of the firms in Sample 1 and Sample 2, this table shows, where applicable, expected recovery rates for the entire firm, senior secured loans, senior unsecured bonds, and senior subordinated bonds as well as standard deviations of respective recovery rates. Figures are averages over the respective observation period. Estimates of implied expected recovery rates are obtained using Eqs. (3.14) and (5.6) – (5.8). Estimates of the standard deviation of implied recovery rates are obtained using Eqs. (3.15) and (C.i) – (C.iii). The estimation approach is specified by Eq. (5.14).

E Implied Recovery Rates by Firm – Sample-Specific Calibration

Sample 1 Constituents

	AMKR	BBY	BYD	COX	DHI	HET	HMA	KBH	MGM	SLR
Firm-Wide Recovery Rate										
Implied Expected	32.8%	38.7%	34.2%	30.8%	31.8%	34.5%	41.2%	33.3%	35.5%	43.4%
Stdev.	30.3%	30.7%	29.6%	30.3%	28.8%	29.7%	31.0%	29.4%	29.9%	30.0%
Recovery Rate of Senior Unsecured Bonds										
Implied Expected	34.1%	39.4%	21.0%	21.6%	19.3%	22.1%	22.3%	22.8%	22.0%	45.5%
Stdev.	37.9%	32.2%	37.9%	32.4%	29.2%	32.9%	37.9%	34.5%	34.4%	31.3%
Recovery Rate of Senior Subordintd Bonds										
Implied Expected	6.5%	1.7%	7.1%	2.7%	0.4%	2.3%	8.4%	3.5%	3.4%	2.0%
Stdev.	19.7%	10.4%	20.2%	10.4%	5.3%	11.9%	22.2%	14.6%	14.6%	11.3%

	STN	TJX	TOL	TRI	TRW	TSO	URI	Avg.
Firm-Wide Recovery Rate								
Implied Expected	29.7%	35.9%	33.6%	42.6%	34.3%	37.7%	35.4%	35.6%
Stdev.	28.5%	30.0%	29.4%	30.6%	29.6%	29.9%	29.8%	29.9%
Recovery Rate of Senior Unsecured Bonds								
Implied Expected	21.9%	32.1%	30.9%	34.2%	20.9%	29.4%	29.3%	27.6%
Stdev.	36.7%	32.8%	34.1%	41.2%	31.0%	34.9%	39.1%	34.7%
Recovery Rate of Senior Subordintd Bonds								
Implied Expected	5.6%	1.5%	2.7%	9.3%	0.8%	2.8%	7.0%	4.0%
Stdev.	17.9%	9.7%	12.9%	23.3%	7.4%	12.3%	20.2%	14.4%

Sample 2 Constituents

	AMD	ARM	AW	CVC	DF	DTV	EP	F	FCX	FSL
Firm-Wide Recovery Rate										
Implied Expected	36.7%	28.5%	26.4%	27.8%	30.6%	30.0%	28.3%	30.1%	35.8%	36.3%
Stdev.	32.9%	31.8%	30.6%	30.8%	32.1%	31.7%	30.9%	31.7%	32.8%	33.5%
Recovery Rate of Senior Secured Loans										
Implied Expected	75.0%	57.5%	49.4%	44.6%	40.5%	53.5%	48.0%	57.5%	65.7%	70.2%
Stdev.	37.8%	43.5%	43.0%	41.2%	39.0%	42.4%	41.4%	42.5%	40.6%	39.9%
Recovery Rate of Senior Unsecured Bonds										
Implied Expected	31.1%	21.2%	9.5%	14.6%	10.5%	19.2%	15.7%	22.5%	26.1%	40.6%
Stdev.	34.1%	31.6%	24.2%	29.2%	25.3%	30.8%	28.4%	33.0%	33.6%	43.2%

	HCA	IDARQ	LEA	MIKE	REAL	SGDS	TRB	TRW	UVN	VSTN	Avg.
Firm-Wide Recovery Rate											
Implied Expected	32.2%	26.8%	29.1%	23.7%	26.9%	29.5%	29.3%	30.9%	28.1%	33.1%	30.0%
Stdev.	32.2%	31.0%	31.8%	29.4%	30.9%	32.0%	31.3%	32.1%	31.2%	32.5%	31.7%
Recovery Rate of Senior Secured Loans											
Implied Expected	48.0%	36.1%	48.8%	38.5%	45.4%	42.3%	49.8%	52.2%	51.7%	60.9%	51.8%
Stdev.	40.9%	38.5%	42.4%	40.5%	41.9%	40.5%	42.2%	42.4%	42.9%	41.7%	41.3%
Recovery Rate of Senior Unsecured Bonds											
Implied Expected	10.7%	9.0%	16.9%	13.3%	14.1%	15.5%	16.8%	19.9%	18.3%	23.5%	18.5%
Stdev.	25.5%	23.7%	29.9%	29.5%	30.3%	32.3%	29.9%	32.8%	30.2%	32.7%	30.5%

For each of the firms in Sample 1 and Sample 2, this table shows, where applicable, expected recovery rates for the entire firm, senior secured loans, senior unsecured bonds, and senior subordinated bonds as well as standard deviations of respective recovery rates. Figures are averages over the respective observation period. Estimates of implied expected recovery rates are obtained using Eqs. (3.14) and (5.6) – (5.8). Estimates of the standard deviation of implied recovery rates are obtained using Eqs. (3.15) and (C.i) – (C.iii). The estimation approach is specified by Eqs. (5.16) and (5.17).

F Implied One-Year Probabilities of Default by Firm

Sample 1 Constituents

	AMKR	BBY	BYD	COX	DHI	HET	HMA	KBH	MGM	SLR
Average	9.1%	0.7%	2.5%	1.5%	1.7%	1.9%	2.4%	2.4%	2.3%	3.2%
Median	8.3%	0.6%	2.3%	1.3%	1.2%	1.0%	1.7%	2.1%	2.1%	3.2%
Max.	21.9%	1.9%	5.7%	6.0%	4.9%	7.0%	4.8%	6.6%	6.1%	3.7%
Min.	3.6%	0.4%	1.4%	0.5%	0.7%	0.6%	1.3%	0.9%	1.5%	2.6%
Standard Deviation	3.8%	0.3%	0.7%	1.1%	1.1%	1.6%	1.2%	1.0%	0.6%	0.4%

	STN	TJX	TOL	TRI	TRW	TSO	URI	Avg.
Average	2.4%	0.4%	1.4%	2.7%	2.8%	1.4%	4.0%	2.5%
Median	2.1%	0.4%	1.2%	2.4%	2.7%	1.3%	3.7%	
Max.	6.6%	0.8%	4.1%	4.0%	5.2%	2.2%	10.2%	
Min.	1.3%	0.2%	0.7%	2.0%	1.7%	1.1%	2.2%	
Standard Deviation	1.0%	0.1%	0.6%	0.5%	0.8%	0.2%	1.7%	1.0%

Sample 2 Constituents

	AMD	ARM	AW	CVC	DF	DTV	EP	F	FCX	FSL
Average	7.0%	8.2%	4.0%	3.5%	4.0%	3.2%	2.5%	9.4%	2.0%	9.7%
Median	5.9%	8.2%	3.7%	2.9%	4.1%	3.4%	2.6%	9.2%	1.9%	10.2%
Max.	12.5%	11.4%	7.3%	7.2%	7.0%	5.6%	4.4%	16.6%	3.0%	16.3%
Min.	4.4%	5.2%	1.9%	1.5%	1.4%	1.4%	1.0%	5.4%	1.6%	3.9%
Standard Deviation	2.3%	1.6%	1.6%	1.5%	1.7%	1.1%	0.9%	3.0%	0.4%	3.2%

	HCA	IDARQ	LEA	MIKE	REAL	SGDS	TRB	TRW	UVN	VSTN	Avg.
Average	4.2%	6.0%	6.3%	4.6%	14.5%	5.1%	8.3%	3.8%	9.1%	10.3%	6.3%
Median	4.4%	4.5%	6.1%	4.8%	11.5%	5.0%	9.1%	3.9%	8.1%	8.7%	
Max.	7.5%	10.9%	10.0%	6.5%	29.6%	8.4%	10.7%	7.7%	15.5%	25.9%	
Min.	1.7%	2.3%	4.2%	2.2%	5.8%	2.8%	4.7%	1.9%	3.7%	4.2%	
Standard Deviation	1.6%	2.9%	1.4%	1.1%	7.1%	1.3%	2.0%	1.4%	3.9%	5.9%	2.3%

For each of the firms in Sample 1 and Sample 2, this table shows key statistics of implied one-year probabilities of default. Figures are obtained using Eq. (5.26).

References

Acharya, Viral, Sreedhar Bharath, and Anand Srinivasan, 2007, Does Industry-wide Distress Affect Defaulted Firms? Evidence from Creditor Recoveries, Journal of Financial Economics, Vol. 85, Issue 3, p787-821.

Altman, Edward, Brooks Brady, Andrea Resti, and Andrea Sironi, 2005, The Link Between Default and Recovery Rates: Theory, Empirical Evidence and Implications, Journal of Business, Vol. 78, Issue 6, p2203-2227.

Altman, Edward and Vellore Kishore, 1996, Almost Everything You Wanted to Know About Recoveries on Defaulted Bonds, Financial Analysts Journal, Vol. 52, Issue 6, p57-64.

Altman, Edward, Andrea Resti, and Andrea Sironi, 2004, Default Recovery Rates in Credit Risk Modelling: A Review of the Literature and Empirical Evidence, Economic Notes, Vol. 33, Issue 2, p183-208.

Artmann, Karin and Martin Bartlam, 2007a, Loan only Credit Default Swaps – The Story so far, Capital Markets Law Journal, Vol. 2, Issue 3, p281-294.

_______, 2007b, Loan only Credit Default Swaps – The New European Standard Form, Capital Markets Law Journal, Vol. 2, Issue 3, p414-426.

Baird, Douglas, Arturo Bris, and Ning Zhu, 2007, The Dynamics of Large and Small Chapter 11 Cases: An Empirical Study, Working Paper.

Bakshi, Gurdip, Dilip Madan, and Frank Zhang, 2006, Understanding the Role of Recovery in Default Risk Models: Empirical Comparison and Implied Recovery Rates, Working Paper.

Basel Committee on Banking Supervision, 2005, Guidance on Paragraph 468 of the Framework Document, Bank for International Settlements, http://www.bis.org.

_______, 2006, International Convergence of Capital Measurement and Capital Standards – A Revised Framework, Bank for International Settlements, http://www.bis.org.

Berd, Arthur, 2005, Recovery Swaps, Journal of Credit Risk, Vol. 1, Issue 2.

Berndt, Antje, Rohan Douglas, Darrel Duffie, Mark Ferguson, and David Schranz, 2005, Measuring Default Risk Premia from Default Swap Rates and EDFs, Working Paper.

Berndt, Antje, Robert Jarrow, and ChoongOh Kang, 2007, Restructuring Risk in Credit Default Swaps: An Empirical Analysis, Stochastic Processes and their Applications, Vol. 177, Issue 11, p1724-1749.

Bharath, Sreedhar and Venky Panchapegesan, 2007, The Changing Nature of Chapter 11, Working Paper.

Bruche, Max and Carlos González-Aguado, 2009, Recovery Rates, Default Probabilities and the Credit Cycle, Journal of Banking and Finance, Vol. 34, Issue 4, p754-764.

Cantor, Richard, Kenneth Emery, and Pamela Stumpp, 2006, Probability of Default Ratings and Loss Given Default Assessments for Non-Financial Speculative-Grade Corporate Obligors in the United States and Canada, Moody's, http://www.moodys.com.

Cantor, Richard and Praveen Varma, 2005, Determinants of Recovery Rates on Defaulted Bonds and Loans for North American Corporate Issuers: 1983-2003, Journal of Fixed Income, Vol. 14, Issue 4, p29-44.

Chamblee, Gary and Jolie Tenholder, 2005, Converging Markets: Leveraged Syndicated Loans and High-Yield Bonds, Commercial Lending Review, Vol. 20, Issue 6, p7-16.

Chava, Sudheer, Catalina Stefanescu, and Stuart Turnbull, 2008, Modeling the Loss Distribution, Working Paper.

Chew, William and Steven Miller, 2007, A Guide to the Loan Market, S&P, http://www.standardandpoors.com.

Christensen, Jens, 2005, Joint Estimation of Default and Recovery Risk: A Simulation Study, Working Paper.

Covitz, Daniel and Song Han, 2004, An Empirical Analysis of Bond Recovery Rates: Exploring a Structural View of Default, Working Paper.

Das, Sanjiv and Paul Hanouna, 2009, Implied Recovery, Journal of Economic Dynamics and Control, Vol. 33, Issue 11, p1837-1857.

Driessen, Joost, 2005, Is Default Event Risk Priced in Corporate Bonds?, Review of Financial Studies, Vol. 18, Issue 1, p165-195.

Duffee, Gregory, 1998, The Relation Between Treasury Yields and Corporate Bond Yield Spreads, Journal of Finance, Vol. 53, Issue 6, p2225-2242.

Duffie, Darrell, 1999, Credit Swap Valuation, Financial Analysts Journal, Vol. 55, Issue 1, p73-87.

Duffie, Darrell and Kenneth Singleton, 1999, Modeling Term Structures of Defaultable Bonds, Review of Financial Studies, Vol. 12, Issue 4, p687-720.

Düllmann, Klaus and Monika Trapp, 2004, Systematic Risk in Recovery Rates – An Empirical Analysis of US Corporate Credit Exposures, Working Paper.

Duncan, Angus, 2006, Loan-only Credit Default Swaps: The March to Liquidity, Commercial Lending Review, Vol. 21, Issue 5, p19-22.

Elizalde, Abel, 2007, Pricing Cancellable LCDS, Merrill Lynch, http://www.ml.com.

Emery, Kenneth, 2007, Moody's Ultimate Recovery Database, Moody's, http://www.moodys.com.

Emery, Kenneth and Sharon Ou, 2004, Credit Loss Rates on Similarly Rated Loans and Bonds, Moody's, http://www.moodys.com.

_______, 2009, Corporate Default and Recovery Rates 1920-2008, Moody's, http://www.moodys.com.

Emery, Kenneth, Sharon Ou, and Jennifer Tennant, 2008, Corporate Default and Recovery Rates 1920-2007, Moody's, http://www.moodys.com.

Ericsson, Jan and Olivier Renault, 2006, Liquidity and Credit Risk, Journal of Finance, Vol. 61, Issue 5, p2219-2250.

Fons, Jerome, 1987, The Default Premium and Corporate Bond Experience, Journal of Finance, Vol. 42, Issue 1, p81-97.

Friedman, Craig and Sven Sandow, 2003, Ultimate Recoveries, Risk Magazine, Vol. 16, Issue 8, p69-73.

Frye, Jon, 2000a, Depressing Recoveries, Risk Magazine, Vol. 13, Issue 11, p108-111.

_______, 2000b, Collateral Damage, Risk Magazine, Vol. 13, Issue 4, p91-94.

_______, 2003, A False Sense of Security, Risk Magazine, Vol. 16, Issue 8, p63-67.

Galiani, Stefano, Alberto Gallo, Jón Jónsson, and Atish Kakodkar, 2006, Credit Derivatives Handbook 2006 – Vol. 1: A Guide to Single-Name and Index CDS Products, Merrill Lynch, http://www.ml.com.

Gaspar, Raquel and Irina Slinko, 2008, On Recovery and Intensity's Correlation – A New Class of Credit Risk Models, Journal of Credit Risk, Vol. 4, Issue 2, p3-35.

Guha, Rajiv, 2003, Recovery of Face Value at Default: Empirical Evidence and Implications for Credit Risk Pricing, Working Paper.

Güntay, Levent, Dilip Madan, and Haluk Unal, 2003, Pricing the Risk of Recovery in Default with Absolute Priority Rule Violation, Journal of Banking and Finance, Vol. 27, Issue 6, p1001-1025.

Gupton, Greg and Roger Stein, 2002, Losscalc™: Model for Predicting Loss Given Default, Moody's, http://www.moodys.com.

Hamilton, David, 2007, Corporate Default and Recovery Rates 1920-2006, Moody's, http://www.moodys.com.

Hamilton, David and Praveen Varma, 2006, Corporate Default and Recovery Rates 1920-2005, Moody's, http://www.moodys.com.

Harding, Paul, 2003, Mastering the ISDA Master Agreements (1992 and 2002): A Practical Guide for Negotiations, 2nd edition, Financial Times Prent. Int, London.

Harpaintner, Stefan, Svetzlozar Rachev, and Stefan Trück, 2005, A Note on Forecasting Aggregate Recovery Rates with Macroeconomic Variables, Working Paper.

Houweling, Patrick and Ton Vorst, 2005, Pricing Default Swaps: Empirical Evidence, Journal of International Money and Finance, Vol. 24, Issue 8, p1200-1225.

Hu, Yen-Ting and William Perraudin, 2002, The Dependence of Recovery Rates and Defaults, Working Paper.

ISDA, 1992, 1992 ISDA Master Agreement, http://www.isda.org.

_______, 2002a, 2002 ISDA Master Agreement, http://www.isda.org.

_______, 2002b, Schedule to the 2002 ISDA Master Agreement, http://www.isda.org.

_______, 2002c, User's Guide to the 2002 ISDA Master Agreement, http://www.isda.org.

_______, 2003, ISDA Credit Derivatives Definitions, http://www.isda.org.

_______, 2006a (June 8), Syndicated Secured Loan Credit Default Swap Standard Terms Supplement, http://www.isda.org.

_______, 2006b (June 8), Confirmation for Use with the Syndicated Secured Loan Credit Default Swap Standard Terms Supplement, http://www.isda.org.

_______, 2007a (May 22), Syndicated Secured Loan Credit Default Swap Standard Terms Supplement, http://www.isda.org.

_______, 2007b (May 22), Confirmation for Use with the Syndicated Secured Loan Credit Default Swap Standard Terms Supplement, http://www.isda.org.

_______, 2007c (July 30), Standard Terms Supplement for Use with Credit Derivative Transactions on Leveraged Loans, http://www.isda.org.

_______, 2007d (July 30), Form of Confirmation for Use with CDS on Leveraged Loans Terms, http://www.isda.org.

_______, 2008a (March 12), Standard Terms Supplement for Use with Credit Derivative Transactions on Leveraged Loans, http://www.isda.org.

_______, 2008b (March 12), Form of Confirmation for Use with CDS on Leveraged Loans Terms, http://www.isda.org.

Janosi, Tibor, Robert Jarrow, and Yildiray Yildirim, 2002, Estimating Expected Losses and Liquidity Discounts Implicit in Debt Prices, Journal of Risk, Vol. 5, Issue 1, p1-38.

Jarrow, Robert and Stuart Turnbull, 1995, Pricing Derivatives on Financial Securities Subject to Credit Risk, Journal of Finance, Vol. 50, Issue 1, p53-85.

Keisman, David, Kevin Kelhoffer, and Jane Zennario, 2004, 2003 Recovery Highlights, S&P, http://www.standardandpoors.com.

Keisman, David, Karen Van de Castle, and Ruth Yang, 2000, Suddenly Structure Mattered: Insights into Recoveries from Defaulted Debt, Standard & Poor's Credit Week, May Issue, p61-68.

Lando, David, 1998, On Cox Processes and Credit Risky Securities, Review of Derivatives Research, Vol. 2, Issue 2-3, p99-120.

Le, Anh, 2007, Separating the Components of Default Risk: A Derivative-based Approach, Working Paper.

Longstaff, Francis, Sanjay Mithal, and Eric Neis, 2005, Corporate Yield Spreads: Default Risk or Liquidity? New Evidence from the Credit Default Swap Market, Journal of Finance, Vol. 60, Issue 5, p2213-2253.

LSTA, 2007 (October 1), User's Guide to the Physical Settlement Rider for Syndicated Secured Loan Credit Default Swaps, http://www.lsta.org.

Madan, Dilip and Haluk Unal, 1998, Pricing the Risks of Default, Review of Derivatives Research, Vol. 2, Issue 2-3, p121-160.

Markit, 2006, Markit RED User Guide, http://www.markit.com.

_______, 2007 (December 4), Syndicated Secured Loan Polling Rules, http://www.markit.com.

May, William, Eric Rosenthal, and Mariarosa Verde, 2007, Stock of Covenant-weak Loans Could Affect Recovery Rates, Fitch, http://www.fitchratings.com.

Pan, Jun and Kenneth Singleton, 2008, Default and Recovery Implicit in the Term Structure of Sovereign CDS Spreads, Journal of Finance, Vol. 63, Issue 5, p2345-2384.

Pykhtin, Michael, 2003, Unexpected Recovery Risk, Risk Magazine, Vol. 16, Issue 8, p74-78.

Renault, Olivier and Olivier Scaillet, 2003, On the Way to Recovery: A Nonparametric Bias Free Estimation of Recovery Rate Densities, Journal of Banking and Finance, Vol. 28, Issue 12, p2915-2931.

Rösch, Daniel and Harald Scheule, 2005, A Multifactor Approach for Systematic Default and Recovery Risk, Journal of Fixed Income, Vol. 15, Issue 2, p63-75.

Saita, Leandro, 2006, The Puzzling Price of Corporate Default Risk, Working Paper.

Schläfer, Timo and Marliese Uhrig-Homburg, 2010a, Syndicated Loans, Loan-only Credit Default Swaps and CDS Legal Documentation, in: Structured Credit Products – Credit Derivatives & Synthetic Securitisation, Moorad Choudhry (editor), 2nd ed., John Wiley & Sons, Singapore.

_______, 2010b, Is Recovery Risk Priced?, Working Paper.

Schneider, Paul, Leopold Sögner, and Tanja Veza, 2009, The Economic Role of Jumps and Recovery Rates in the Market for Corporate Default Risk, forthcoming in: Journal of Financial and Quantitative Analysis.

Solomon, Russel, 2006, Loss Given Default Analytics: User's Guide to Prioritizing Claims and Applying the LGD Model, Moody's, http://www.moodys.com.

_______, 2007, Bank Loan Recoveries and the Role that Covenants Play: What Really Matters?, Moody's, http://www.moodys.com.

Song, Jeong, 2008, Loss Given Default Implied by Cross-sectional No Arbitrage, Working Paper.

Zhang, Frank, 2003, What Did the Credit Market Expect of Argentina Default? Evidence from Default Swap Data, Working Paper.

Zhang, Zhipeng, 2009, Recovery Rates and Macroeconomic Conditions: The Role of Loan Covenants, Working Paper.

MIX
Papier aus verantwortungsvollen Quellen
Paper from responsible sources
FSC® C105338

If you have any concerns about our products,
you can contact us on
ProductSafety@springernature.com

In case Publisher is established outside the EU,
the EU authorized representative is:
Springer Nature Customer Service Center GmbH
Europaplatz 3, 69115 Heidelberg, Germany

Printed by Libri Plureos GmbH
in Hamburg, Germany